D1064694

Celebrating Canada

Decorating with History in a Contemporary Home

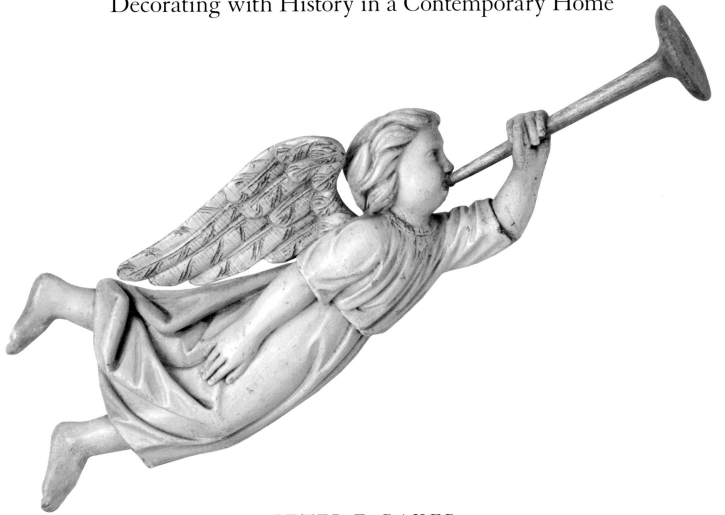

PETER E. BAKER

Photography by Marc Bider

DUNDURN
TORONTO

This book is published with financial support from the following Canadian corporations:

GardaWorld   TransCanada PipeLines   PWL Capital
Telus   Power Corporation of Canada

Page design/layout: Kim Monteforte, WeMakeBooks.ca
Cover image: Marc Bider
Printer: Friesens

Library and Archives Canada Cataloguing in Publication

Baker, Peter E., author
Celebrating Canada: decorating with history in a contemporary home /
Peter E. Baker; photography by Marc Bider.

Includes bibliographical references and index.
Issued in print and electronic formats.

ISBN 978-1-4597-4032-7 (hardcover)
ISBN 978-1-4597-4033-4 (PDF)
ISBN 978-1-4597-4025-9 (EPUB)

1. Antiques—Canada. 2. Folk art—Canada. 3. Decoration and ornament,
Rustic—Canada. 4. Interior decoration—Canada. I. Title.

NK841.B35 2017   745.0971   C2017-901079-4
                                          C2017-901080-8

We acknowledge the support of the **Canada Council for the Arts** and the **Ontario Arts Council** for our publishing program. We also acknowledge the financial support of the Government of Ontario, through the **Ontario Book Publishing Tax Credit** and the **Ontario Media Development Corporation**, and the **Government of Canada**.

Care has been taken to trace the ownership of copyright material used in this book. The author and the publisher welcome any information enabling them to rectify any references or credits in subsequent editions.

— *J. Kirk Howard, President*

The publisher is not responsible for websites or their content unless they are owned by the publisher.

Printed and bound in Canada.

VISIT US AT

dundurn.com | @dundurnpress | dundurnpress | dundurnpress

Dundurn
3 Church Street, Suite 500
Toronto, Ontario, Canada
M5E 1M2

Celebrating Canada

Decorating with History in a Contemporary Home

PETER E. BAKER

Photography by Marc Bider

DUNDURN
TORONTO

CANADIAN MUSEUM OF HISTORY
MUSÉE CANADIEN DE L'HISTOIRE

Table of Contents

Foreword 9

Preface 11

Introduction. 15

The Entrance 21

   Diamond Point Doors 22

   Neoclassic Pine Corner Cupboard 24

   Walking Stick — Ancienne Lorette 26

   Mi'kmaq Quillwork 28

   Frederick S. Barnjum — Painter 30

Living Room 39

   Chantecler Weathervane. 40

   French Régime Armchair 42

   Drum Table 46

   Niagara Falls — Robert Whale 48

   Draught Horses. 50

   Diamond Point Armoire. 52

   A View of Dundas — J.R. Seavey 54

   Damase Richard 56

   Northwest Coast Motif Blanket Chest 60

Library. 63

   Tiger Maple Corner Cupboard. 64

   1837 Rebellion Box. 66

   Carved Brush 68

   Abenaki Deed Boxes. 72

   John Tulles Card Table. 76

   John Tulles Side Chair 80

   Holland Landing Red Mill 82

   Jean-Baptiste Côté — "L'habitant" 84

   New Brunswick "Nisbet" Sewing Table 86

   Bird Sculptures — Jean-Baptiste Côté 88

   Stevens Family Portraits. 94

   Newfoundland Keepsake Box. 96

   Death of Wolfe 98

   McGee Table 100

   Joseph Romuald Bernier — Lumberman 102

   Beaver Crooked Knife. 104

   Portage in the Fog — F.A. Hopkins 106

   Exploring New Lands — Journals of Mackenzie and Weld . . . 108

Dining Room/Kitchen 111

    The Huron Box *112*

    Convent Boxes *114*

    Seminary Parrot *120*

    Three-Tier Chandelier *122*

    S.J. Doyle/J.A. Mahar Trade Sign 124

    Carved Figure of Napoleon *126*

    Louis XV Armoire *128*

    Fruit Vendor Trade Sign. *130*

    Fort Duquesne Game Board *132*

Bedrooms/Bathrooms 135

    Hooked Rug — Laurentian Village. *136*

    Silas Patterson Heart Table *138*

    Decorated Canoe Paddle. *140*

    Hooked Rugs *142*

    Miss Madilla Smith — E.S., Painter *150*

    Quebec Chest of Drawers *152*

    Thomas Nisbet Legislative Desk *154*

    Josefina *156*

    Halifax Dressing Table *158*

    Horse and Buggy — Punkeydoodles Corners. *160*

    Longpré Bird Shelf. *162*

    Timber Shanty *164*

    Logging Scene — Julius Hümme *166*

    Carved Deer *168*

    Main Street, Winnipeg — E.J. Hutchins *170*

    The Steamship S.S. Quebec *172*

    Indian Mother and Hunter — D. Gale *174*

Mud Room/Stairwell 177

    Norfolk County Buffet. *178*

    Canadian Shorebirds. *180*

    Bakery Trade Sign — J. Bourgault *186*

    Game Boards *188*

Family Room/Den 207

    Captain Robert Chestnut *208*

    Hooked Rugs — Deanne Fitzpatrick. *210*

    Manitoba Pheasant. *214*

    Horse Pull Toy *216*

    Beaver Weathervane. *218*

    The Fenian Raids. *220*

    Recruitment Posters *224*

Acknowledgements. 227

Select Bibliography 229

Index 235

"Yet, collectors as committed as the one described by Maupassant also believe that objects are meant to be passed on, their value stemming less from their inherent market valuation than from their circulation, the mysterious ways in which they have touched, in turn, multiple lives. They are silent witnesses, sentinels of our lives. They have stories to tell."

"A Passion for Bibelot"
Yaëlle Azagury
Jerusalem Post, 2011

Foreword

In the table of contents for this new book, Peter Baker, collector, appraisal expert, long-time dealer and enthusiast, proposes a broad array of objects, historical events, anecdotes, and stories, in a call to the celebration of Canada's 150th birthday, through a fresh and amusing opening into the material history of our country and the discovery of its hidden potential for renewal. In the role of objects as active players in our everyday lives, these are the only real "events" of the past that survive in direct material form to awaken and expose the thick textures of experience, cultural environs, and our identity in the present.

Choosing a room-by-room path through the house of avid collectors Joan and Derek Burney, Baker has borrowed an appropriate procedure from historical inventory practices in Quebec, in order to establish a coherent domestic geography to guide the reader into the spaces and corners of the furnishings, accessories, and material constituents that recall to us our own environments. The concept of a single collection, anchored in the passage of more than 300 years of common history in all its material diversity, reclaims the years and objects represented here, exceptionally focused, and repurposed in delightful and surprising ways.

Peter Baker's presentation, loaded with aesthetic and technical details, humorous and subtle juxtapositions, and a seemingly impartial political subtext to punctuate the narrative, slides smoothly along story lines of objects that remind us of some of the tragic and tender moments of our recorded history: a painting of the battle of the Plains of Abraham; the Rebellion box of William Alves dated 1838, "a kind mementoe" to Miss Sophia Kelly; Macdonald and Laurier in sculpted wood, paint, and ceramic squaring off across the entry to the House.

This is a book for everyone because it reveals and defines the hidden importance of objects in the creation of historical narrative, the record of communities, practices, and individual identities through the debris of daily living or, as some have suggested, a kind of "history from below."

John A. Fleming
Toronto, Ontario

Naive carved deed box, Quebec, early 19th century.

Preface

Our decision to start this journey with Peter Baker as author was influenced by two factors: first, to help celebrate Canada's 150th anniversary by sharing the history of objects that we are fortunate to have under our care, and, second, to inspire in some small way the collecting of Canadiana by a new generation of Canadians. Our primary contribution has been to provide the backdrop, the featured examples; our reasoning in so doing is simple — to share and to help inspire the passion.

For Christmas in the 1970s we bought a sap-gathering bucket in red paint and a wonderful book by Jean and Elizabeth Smith entitled *Collecting Canada's Past* — these two items reflected both the beginning of our commitment to Canadiana and, with a family of four boys, the limit of family finances.

This new world of antiques gradually opened up due to the kindness of other young buyers willing to share their experience and the patience of dealers who took time to engage those of us who showed early symptoms of passion, even if we weren't quite ready to buy. But it wasn't long before we made our third investment in antiques — "Little Bob's Skating Lamp" — which I desperately needed because my mother had used one on a frozen prairie pond.

These memories are mentioned only as a reminder that if we wish to encourage younger generations to participate or even to develop the curiosity to wonder about Canadiana and antiques in general, then there must be exposure to the product. Passion is contagious, but, as in the case of all "diseases", there first must be contact.

For collectors, the health of the antiques industry is as important as it is for the professionals involved, and it seems to depend in part on the excitement generated in the marketplace. This energy stems from the support we collectors offer to all the players (dealers, pickers, show promoters, auction houses, and other collectors) and our willingness to attempt to explain our particular passion to others.

It has been said that it takes a village to raise a child; similarly, it is the professional antique community that allows for the creation of any collection — a collection after all being an assemblage of already collected items from which we, as collectors, choose. For example, the objects in the library on page 63 were sourced from fourteen different dealers, although one item is hidden behind the bottom cupboard doors! Our village is indeed well populated.

We are fortunate in this country to have two magazines dedicated to our shared interest, and each with a completely different perspective and function. *The Upper Canadian* was redefined as *Canadian Antiques & Vintage* magazine, repositioned by Sophie and J. Herbert Bond, to serve the needs and interests of the larger collecting community, but still with regular coverage of Canadiana in all its forms. The second magazine is *Ornamentum, Decorative Arts in Canada*, where a decorative art is described as "a creative work, frequently of a practical or useful nature produced by an artist, craftsman, or amateur which has intrinsic aesthetic and/or historical value." I read each issue with a sense of discovery and wonder!

Everyone has a mental list of those who had an influence in informing taste and standards (influenced of course by collecting genre, geography, availability, and even personalities); in the next few paragraphs we wish to present our own particular fellow "villagers" as they pertain to this Canadiana collection. Without these professionals it would have been impossible to find and acquire such diverse and unique objects to decorate our home.

A few years ago John A. Fleming and Michael Rowan wrote a superb and informative magnum opus called *Canadian Folk Art to 1950* (published in 2012), an extensive and scholarly record of our material and cultural history. Their effort generated great enthusiasm in our collecting community and their definition of folk art with their sophisticated approach to celebrating the "aesthetic of the everyday" helps to clarify an area of collecting that can be extremely difficult to explain.

The effort of Henry and Barbara Dobson in publishing *Heritage Furnishings of Atlantic Canada* in 2010 is of equal importance to a different group of collectors as was the role Henry played in educating anyone with the interest and passion to learn. Henry passed away at 91 after a lifetime of scholarly devotion to the study of formal Canadian furnishings — "all based on the principles of 18th and early 19th century Classicism," he liked to say. Henry and Barbara's generosity in sharing their knowledge (and lunches) on a continuing basis offered a distinct perspective, encouraging us to expand our collecting horizons.

As a mentor, there is one outstanding American collector and a dear friend, Martha Bartlett, who provided me with the equivalent of a personal four-year intensive course on antiques and folk art with a "pop quiz" at unexpected intervals. She prefers, and indeed insists on, being called a decorator because no matter how wonderful an object may be according to her own high standard, if it will not show well in her home, it must not be purchased — discipline being the key. After remarking that the items observed on our many forays were all Americana, her reply was: "Excellence is excellence. Learn here and then buy when you go home." It was great advice and she continues (being only in her tenth decade) to vigorously comb her marketplace for items of Canadiana for us of which there have been several great finds.

Our personal village also houses Ruth Stalker Antiques, a successful storefront operation begun decades ago by Ruth, a strong entrepreneurial woman with a passion for Canadiana that never faltered, making every encounter with her a pleasure. Sadly Ruth passed away in 2016 but not before learning about the planned release of *Celebrating Canada*, a project she endorsed to the core. There is nothing like a shared passion to cement a friendship. It seems to also cement a family, as children Alison and Jamie proudly build upon Ruth's legacy with a business that accelerated in a large measure our journey of collecting Canadiana.

And we cannot speak of Canadiana without mentioning Gerard Bourguet, "Éminence Grise", who for many years has set high standards for the collecting of early Quebec furniture and furnishings, frequently offering exceptional objects rarely seen on the marketplace.

There are antique dealers all across Canada who warrant a visit, as well as dealer and auction sites, discussion groups, and forums found on the Web. In our small collecting niche we are grateful to several individuals for their patience, passion and contribution to both our particular collection and the antiques industry.

The list begins with those previously mentioned above and also includes, among others: Carol and Clay Benson, Steven Blevins and Sonja Morawetz, Serge Brouillard, George Brown, Cathy Consentino, Brian Davies, Judy Dawson, Bill Dobson and Linda Hynes, Barry Ezrin, Larry Foster, David and Mary Jo Field, Tim and Liz Isaac, Wendy Hamilton, Leo Kessels (upholsterer), Jean Lafrance, Don Lake, Jose

Lopez, Patrick McGahern, Bill Pinkney and David Keough, Tim and Gerda Potter, Philip Ross, Margaret Ruhland, Bob and Brenda Starr, Carol Telfer, Andre and Claire Vachet, Michel Prince, and Ted Williams.

And we can't conclude without mentioning the author of this book, Peter Baker, who came to our notice highly recommended by American collectors with whom he was doing business at shows in the United States. Thus began a close association that has gradually influenced our focus on what could be termed a "sculptural" approach to individual pieces. In fact Peter's advertisements carry a common theme: *Decorate with Distinction*. His eye for form and the elegance of simplicity reminded my husband Derek and me of a term we learned while living and working in Japan in the 1960s — *shibui*, a Japanese term that has no precise synonym in English or French. With a family immersion in our host culture for over eight years, we all learned about *shibui*. It is a particular aesthetic concept that is difficult to explain, much like defining folk art; in basic terms *shibui* defines beauty as simple, subtle, but complex. Interestingly it seems that Peter arrived at a similar place in his thinking but by a different, authentically Canadian route.

With the 150th anniversary of Canada upon us we must celebrate our history in a spirit of gratitude and appreciation. Respect for our material heritage is an essential part of understanding our history and thus ourselves. We leave you now to the expertise of Peter Baker with a cautionary comment to the novice collector with some words written in 1883:

"The man smitten by an antique is a lost man" — French author Guy de Maupassant

May the passion never stop.

Joan Burney
Ottawa, Ontario

Introduction

—— 🍁 ——

This is a book about living with "soul", about giving a contemporary home a unique identity in a time when immediate fulfillment and peer acceptance pervade social media and where history is frequently viewed as something best left to academics and the stuffy living rooms of elderly relatives. Inspired by the 150th anniversary of Canadian Confederation in 2017 — the same year recognizing 375 years of settlement in Montreal — the goal is to renew awareness towards the material history that surrounds us no matter where we may live in Canada. In these pages we show how antiques and folk art can work with a modern lifestyle, imparting an ambience impossible to achieve with the furniture and decorative accessories available at the nearest big box store.

Not a "period" restoration where objects are selected purely on a narrowly defined moment in time, the featured collection of Joan and Derek Burney represents objects spanning three centuries of Canadian history, from the early days of French settlement to the inspired creativity of late 20th century folk artists. With illustrated items ranging from examples that could be easily found on the market today to highly sought museum quality pieces, it is hoped that both seasoned collectors and those new to the world of antiques and folk art will be challenged to explore new avenues in making the home an even more interesting and dynamic living space.

Each profiled piece reminds us of the strength of character and ingenuity that built this country. From the imaginative output of the rural folk artist who literally whittled away his time during the long cold winters, to the classic forms created by academically trained cabinet makers, Canada has produced a wealth of artistic treasures that all too often have earned more respect and appreciation from our neighbours to the south. Several significant pieces featured have been repatriated from the United States including the French Régime Armchair featured on page 42, the Seminary Parrot on page 120 and the Three-Tier Chandelier on pages 14 and 122.

One of my early encounters with Joan Burney was in my booth at the Bonaventure Antique Show in Montreal where she came in with another friend/collector. We soon bonded over Madilla Smith, the portrait of a young girl featured on page 151. As we discussed the merits of the painting and other items presented for sale I realized that this person was not just decorating, she and her husband Derek were chasing history, looking for the Canadian story behind the piece. Who made it? When? Where? Why?

The portrait of Madilla was of interest not only because of the innocent charm captured by the artist, but also because it came with some clues and an oral provenance of being found in an old Ontario homestead. Who was Madilla? Who was *E.S., Painter*? Could this be a portrait by an unknown early 19th century Canadian artist? These were all questions I had asked myself, however, in pre-Internet days it was too time-consuming for me to easily investigate. But with Joan's purchase of Madilla the real research began and so did an enduring friendship of respect and a shared passion for unearthing the Canadian story and playing a part in preserving our collective past.

Despite our close proximity, Canadian antiques are often very distinct from their American counterparts. Partially due to geography and remote settlement, partially due to the relative isolation of groups based on

CHAPTER 1

❧

The Entrance

As you enter the home you are greeted by two of Canada's early prime ministers: straight ahead nestled in the neoclassic corner cupboard is Sir John A. Macdonald, Conservative, the country's first prime minister, 1867-73, 1878-91, and, appropriately, to the left, stands Sir Wilfrid Laurier, Liberal, the country's first French-Canadian prime minister, 1896-1911.

Laurier

At the foot of the stairs on a mahogany table is a sculpture of Wilfrid Laurier in a statesman-like pose but with a folky charm in his stance and an agreeable disposition in his face. Carved in pine by Joseph Pelletier, Saint-Lin, Quebec, the carving is naive yet well executed with strong detail in the ruffled shirt, vest, jacket and leg garters. The sculpture retains its original polychrome paint and rests on a painted marbleized base.

Dated on the bottom, 1873, one year before Laurier began his record 45 years serving in the House of Commons, making him 32 years old at the time. Wilfrid Laurier grew up in Saint-Lin, the same village as the carver Pelletier, so it is most likely that the two men were acquainted, perhaps this sculpture was a prophecy of great things to come for the politician to be.

Provenance: Estate of Alan Clairman, Toronto.

In the pine corner cupboard is a commemorative plate featuring John A. Macdonald sitting in a relaxed pose with his walking stick across his lap, subtly positioned to keep an eye on Wilfrid Laurier in the opposite corner of the entrance.

Although unmarked, this plate is of English manufacture in the 1880s, transfer printed and identical in size, shape, and age to a commemorative plate of Edward Blake, Macdonald's Liberal opponent in parliament from 1879 to 1887. Canada's coat of arms from the 1880 period is printed above the image, while a cartouche below identifies the sitter.

The history of commemorative images of Canadian notable figures dates back to the end of the 18th century. With new production techniques, a vast array of transfer print Canadian historic scenes and commemorative plates were produced in different colours from a variety of English and Scottish factories through the 19th century.

Macdonald

DIAMOND POINT DOORS

A pair of doors may seem an unusual choice for decorating the staircase wall in the front hall, but the powerful presence of these Quebec armoire doors immediately transforms them into sculpture, enhanced by the pewter-blue paint and three deeply cut classic diamond point panels on each door.

Early houses often had built-in cupboards with panelled or carved doors, but to find a house with interior trim intact is a rarity. Generations of renovations sent the doors to the attic or, worse, the burn pile, making the survivors rarer still. Other doors are found on the market that were once part of an armoire or cupboard, the cupboard left behind because it was considered to be scrap or too bulky to move. The early pickers had an enormous choice and were simply responding to demand as the city dealers had many customers wanting armoire doors for everything from built-in cabinets to headboards for the beds.

Many exceptional doors were stripped of their original paint as per the fashion of the day, but some, like this pair in the stairwell, have survived intact to successfully serve a new purpose as decorative art. The original fiche hinges, hand-forged door escutcheon, and overall form, along with the wear pattern and construction details, date the doors to the 1760-1780 period.

NEOCLASSIC PINE CORNER CUPBOARD

In the front entrance is a small pine corner cupboard with a glazed upper section displaying a beaver bowl in colour and a few examples of sponge decorated "Portneuf" pottery including a porridge bowl with a rooster motif, a pitcher with a deer, and plates with butterflies or nesting birds. Portneuf is a colloquial term for this type of sponge-decorated utilitarian pottery exported to Quebec from Scotland in the late nineteenth century.

Some will admire this cupboard not only for its form but also for its clean natural pine patina, the original faux mahogany surface having been carefully removed several decades ago. From a purist collector point-of-view, the lack of original paint on this cupboard is significant; however, the exuberant execution of the carved details and its overall form and rarity cannot be overlooked. Collectors of original paint should not be so rigid as to deny themselves the pleasure of owning a great piece of classic Canadiana refinished years ago by instead purchasing a mid-range piece in paint for the same price.

This cupboard successfully incorporates an array of Neoclassic "Adam" architectural features that includes a broken-arch carved pediment — a rarity in Canadian furniture — as well as columns, arches, fluting, beading, rosettes, and ovals. In Canadian furniture it also typically includes the notched dentil cornice and linen-fold panel (hollow cut corners), either carved or created with fine mouldings. The single lattice glazed upper door is above two raised panel doors in finely executed Neoclassic style

The lower section of this one-piece cupboard has two linen-fold panel doors over a bracket base shaped in a simple provincial Chippendale style. The side returns are adorned with two vertical architectural panels topped by a carved rosette, a motif that is also found in the horizontal band at the waist with alternating fluted bars.

The geometric glazing pattern in the upper section draws your attention to the contents. Elongated panels adorn the side returns and the reeded frieze of the top section is surmounted by a moulding topped by the broken arch pediment terminating in carved rosettes. The deep relief carving of the pediment includes a ribbon edge that further defines the cut-out profile. Hardware consists of cast "pin and barrel" hinges and brass knobs on the doors.

An exquisite piece of furniture.

Found in North Hatley, Quebec, 1790-1810.

WALKING STICK — ANCIENNE LORETTE

There are many kinds of allegorical walking sticks in collections — some seem to be a random assemblage of myths and whimsy, some are decorated with religious symbolism, some with dogs or birds, while others seem to tell a long-lost story.

Important family provenance from the picker who found this carved stick in a house in Ste-Anne-de-Bellevue, Quebec, revealed its origins to be in the village of Ancienne Lorette. Today this is a part of Quebec City where, in 1674, the Jesuit priest Pierre-Joseph-Marie Chaumonot constructed a brick church — *La Chapelle Notre Dame de Lorette* — after fleeing with a group of Huron from the Midland area of Ontario to escape the warring Iroquois.

This walking stick relates this story of the Huron in Ancienne Lorette.

Ever inquisitive, our intrepid collectors took a road trip to the site that proved invaluable in uncovering the walking stick's history — in a small museum inside a new church built on the same site is a model of the original *Chapelle Notre Dame de Lorette*. The original chapel had been enlarged in 1835 and remained standing until 1907, some 230 years later, until the new church was constructed.

The original chapel bell tower is replicated in the top section of the walking stick, naively crafted but intricate in conceptualization. The pommel is topped by a carved ball on the shingled roof with a carved chantecler on one side of the tower and the large bell wheel on the other. Through the window grill is the black bell, while a bell ringer hangs precariously on the ledge as if he is backing away from the noise. The tower is delineated to simulate bricks or cut stone, just like the original chapel, with the lower section incorporating a "balls in cage" whimsy — a feature found on many walking sticks of the folk genre.

Dominating the main body of the cane is a serpent with a fully carved polychrome Native female figure on the opposite side, the two being joined in only three places. The serpent's head reaches up to the bell tower base with tongue flickering on the brick while a dove of peace and a frog are found on the other two sides. The serpent terminates with a small "ball in cage" rattlesnake tail and the opposite side features a spotted salamander whose tail is being bitten by a bear. In First Nations symbology the salamander is often associated with transformation — in this case perhaps referring to the Hurons' conversion to the Jesuit religion. At the end of the stick the carver has left his initials CMF over a circle of four dancing figures painted red and blue: two British soldiers and two women dancing hand in hand.

Now more than a great folky cane, this walking stick tells the story of Ancienne Lorette — from its Huron beginnings to their acceptance of Christianity with the Jesuits and the transfer of power to the British — ironically, it could have been made in celebration of Confederation a mere 150 years ago....

Carved by CMF, Ancienne Lorette, Quebec, circa 1860.

MI'KMAQ QUILLWORK

Why are there panels of Native Canadian quillwork (flattened and dyed porcupine quills) on a 19th century mahogany Scottish chair?

Although quill decoration can be found in other regions, a prolific number of objects were produced by the Mi'kmaq of New Brunswick, Nova Scotia, Quebec's Gaspé, Prince Edward Island, Newfoundland, and parts of northeastern New England.

Using quills as decorative material, generally in geometric motifs, dates to the early settlement period of North America when the first Europeans reported seeing exquisite quill decorated costumes on the local indigenous people (Beothuk, Maliseet, and Mi'kmaq). Accounts from the early 1600s show that the Mi'kmaq were already trading quill-decorated hide garments to seasonal European fisherman along the coast.

Working with quills is a time consuming task that was generally assigned to the women who would soften the quills with their saliva before flattening them with their teeth and then immersing them in

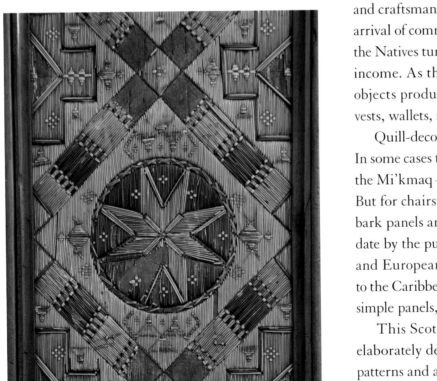

natural dyes. Earlier pieces can often be identified not only by the style and craftsmanship but also by a more limited colour palette before the arrival of commercial dyes around 1860. With the influx of Europeans the Natives turned to making quillwork boxes as a means of trade and income. As the popularity of quillwork grew so did the variety of objects produced, which eventually included purses, pin cushions, vests, wallets, napkin rings, and wall plaques.

Quill-decorated furniture began to appear by the mid 19th century. In some cases the furniture was created in birch bark and decorated by the Mi'kmaq — objects such as cradles, log carriers, and work boxes. But for chairs and tables the Mi'kmaq created quill-decorated birch bark panels and sold them as-is, to be turned into furniture at a later date by the purchaser. Many of these panels were acquired by sailors and European visitors and taken back to England, France, or even to the Caribbean where examples have been found. Some remained as simple panels, serving as wall hangings for many years.

This Scottish or Irish chair shows a T-shape back panel quite elaborately decorated with quillwork in both vertical and diagonal patterns and a geometric starfish motif in the centre. The intricacy of the design, and the style of chair with its carved back crest and spiral twist posts, suggests a date in the 1840-1870 period. There is some quill loss, especially to the seat with the original birch bark under-layer being exposed, but the overall effect of the design speaks for itself.

A dramatic combination of two cultures.

FREDERICK S. BARNJUM — PAINTER

At first glance one might think of Cornelius Krieghoff when looking at these paintings, but examination reveals them as the work of Frederick Samuel Barnjum, a lesser-known contemporary of Krieghoff, but a master nonetheless for his own renditions of life in rural Quebec in the mid-19th century. The Barnjum paintings presented here are notable for their perspective and attention to detail, but still retaining a naive charm; his precision with form is most evident in the horses that are treated with equal or even greater importance than the people in the scenes.

Although listed as an artist in the Montreal Directory between 1858 and 1887, the active time period is considerably reduced in *Early Painters and Engravers in Canada* by J. Russell Harper where Barnjum describes himself as an artist for only eight years, from 1858 through 1866. Perhaps he continued painting as a hobby, but his career took a different turn after that, explaining why very few paintings by Frederick Barnjum have surfaced on the public market.

Known works are of genre Quebec scenes and landscapes, in both watercolour and oil. All appear to be of the Montreal area and are generally winter scenes depicting horses, sleighs, carts, and people, with habitations barely visible in the distance. These examples show excellent detail where the people depicted are natural in posture compared to the exuberance found in many Krieghoff scenes.

Barnjum captures the movement and conformation of the horses with ease, showing them meticulously groomed with elaborate harness and feather tassels hanging from their bridles. In several paintings the same driver appears with his mutton-chop facial hair and sporting a typical "habitant" sash around his waist; his female passenger appears in the identical coat and cap, while the attendant wears a red scarf and a Cossack style hat. Is it the same couple out of convenience, or is it a series of self-portraits of Frederick Barnjum and his wife experiencing the scenes first-hand?

Barnjum's affinity for art and anatomy took him to a new career in 1866 as a professor of physical culture and operator of a gymnasium and school for culture and art. An important historical figure in Montreal history, in the 1880s Frederick Barnjum became the first teacher of physical education at McGill University and his sister Helen was the first female instructor. Barnjum's good friend James Naismith took over as director of physical training at McGill in 1889; two years later, the Canadian Naismith invented the game of basketball.

Frederick S. Barnjum miniatures, watercolour.

A rare summer scene by Frederick Barnjum with details of Quebec habitant life such as the double-decker stove in the cabin from Forge du Saint-Maurice, the clay pipe in the hat band, and the Mohawk baskets with the ladies.

Examples of works by Frederick S. Barnjum can be found in collections at the Vancouver Art Gallery, the Art Gallery of Greater Victoria, and Library and Archives Canada (formerly in the Jules Loeb collection, Gatineau, Quebec).

CHAPTER 2

Living Room

Just as in houses of the 18th century where a common room predominated with a fireplace, seating, cooking, and dining facilities all in one room, the living room of this late 20th century home is part of a large open space that also includes the dining area and kitchen.

Early Quebec furniture dominates the living room, which also includes select pieces of folk art and, hanging over the fireplace, an iconic Canadian view of Niagara Falls painted by Ontario artist Robert Whale.

CHANTECLER WEATHERVANE

From his perch atop the armoire, the chantecler is master of his domain, surveying the room like a proud sentinel, chest puffed and head held high, mimicking his youth of some 175 years ago as he overlooked the village square.

Weathervanes have existed in some form for thousands of years as a tool for predicting wind direction and strength. The earliest recorded example dates from 48 BCE in Athens, where a half man/half fish sculpture of the Greek god Triton was erected by the astronomer Andronicus. The sculptural value of such a visually prominent symbol was recognized very early on, limited only by imagination, resulting in weathervanes of animals, mythical figures, trade symbols, and flag-type banners. But by the 9th century CE, it is the rooster that dominates the Christian world as a weathervane symbol, following an edict from Pope Nicolas advocating a cockerel adorn every church to remind people of Peter's initial betrayal of Christ and his subsequent devotion. In Quebec the chantecler atop the church steeple also represented a nostalgic connection to the French roots of the parish.

The familiarity of the rooster as a church symbol and its natural position as barnyard king made the weathercock a predominant choice in North America, atop barns, steeples, public buildings, and homes. As industrialization lowered costs and improved manufacturing output, weathervanes became accessible to a wider market, selling in the late 19th century from a few dollars to fifty dollars for a premium copper example. During this period a vast array of designs were available, but in rural Quebec the popularity of the noble rooster remained unchallenged.

This hand-wrought chantecler is a unique example, constructed and soldered in full-body with an applied comb, wings, and cut tail, all originally surfaced with gold paint. The maker has successfully captured the essence of the rooster with its large fan tail and full chest, emphasized by the strategic placement of the legs towards the rear of the body. The graceful lines flow from the tail, under the belly, up the neck, and terminate at the beak, all in one continuous S-curve; the original wattles are intact as is the prominent comb, although the tips have suffered from the elements. The feet are missing. Several factors indicate an original use atop a church steeple: the large size, the gold painted surface, and the fact that it was never painted over, suggest that it was perched high in the sky indeed.

In untouched, as-found condition, with strong remnants of the original gold paint, exceptional form.

Quebec, mid-19th century.

FRENCH RÉGIME ARMCHAIR

"Les Anglais arrivent!" exclaimed the seigneur as he discussed the possible fate of New France with neighbours that night in September 1759. The high back of his chair was of comfort as he laid back in thought, while the substantial descending arms provided ample support for his firm grip as the discussion grew more heated …

The stories this chair could tell. Created for a member of the elite in New France several decades prior to the Battle of Quebec, this armchair or *fauteuil* is a rare survivor of the French Régime period. Following the defining battle on the Plains of Abraham, life and styles started to change in the colony. As upper class taste adapted to the times, a chair like this may have been shunted aside in favour of a newer English model. Somehow, this chair found its way to the United States where its sloping arms were hidden and upholstered to replicate a later lolling chair with long flat arms. The *Black Beauty* story continues as the armchair was then draped in Victorian upholstery with tassels around the seat, then eventually donated to an American museum, where its bold turnings suggested an American William and Mary period armchair. With time comes knowledge, and the Museum eventually deaccessioned the chair to be sold at auction, where it

was catalogued as a 17th century European Flemish armchair. Seen in an American ad by a keen-eyed friend, the chair was rescued from its plight, coming home to its rightful place as a fine example of early French Canadian furniture.

In classic Louis XIII rectilinear form with a straight crest rail, a strongly canted back continuing from the chamfered rear legs and finely turned stretchers and legs, the sculptural quality of this chair cannot be denied.

Portions of the original ball feet are still intact, albeit with height loss on all four legs as a result of over three hundred years of use. The elaborately turned undercarriage epitomizes strength and sophistication, with the vase, ball, and ring turnings interrupted by elongated cubes at the double-pegged joints. Massive by today's standards, the graceful descending arms are positioned midway on the back posts, terminating in a boldly carved handgrip featuring finger grooves and simply carved spiral ram's horn profiles. The arm post is a continuation of the front leg turned in the same vase, ball, and ring form. Incredibly, this armchair retains its original dark surface, likely stained to resemble walnut as would have been the fashion at home in France. This was a chair created for the elite; more simple variations of the form were created up to the mid-19th century and are readily available on the market — interesting for their vernacular and individual interpretation of the style.

Reupholstered in period-style indigo resist-dyed cotton with black moss and horsehair cushioning salvaged during restoration, minor repairs primarily related to insensitive earlier upholsterers, the chair is structurally intact and sound, pegged construction, birch, in original paint and varnished surface.

Quebec, 1690-1720.

DRUM TABLE

Positioned as a side table beside the French Régime armchair is a rare country example of a drum table, an English form generally found in finer hard woods and more sophisticated style. Although almost 150 years apart in date, the simplicity and stature of this table is a perfect complement to the robust turnings and overall presence of the armchair.

Constructed in white pine with a circular top and banded edge, the table has four Regency inspired legs affixed to a robust chamfered pedestal, all in the original red/brown surface, painted to look like the mahogany of its richer cousins. The "drum" skirt retains four curved drawers with their original pulls and nailed joinery. There is shrinkage of the round top that is a natural occurrence as wood contracts laterally over time. This is one thing experts look for in authenticating round top tables, which, in this case, has caused the one-inch circular band to separate from the edge in spots — a helpful indication of age and authenticity.

Quebec, 1830-1850.

NIAGARA FALLS — ROBERT WHALE

Above the mantelpiece in the living room is an oil painting of Niagara Falls painted by Robert Whale of Burford, Ontario. Flanked by a pair of carved horses that appear ready to march into the picture, the effect is three dimensional as the perspective of the painting draws you in.

Robert Whale (1805-1887) was born in Cornwall, England, emigrating to Burford in 1852 and subsequently to Brantford in 1864. With his ambitions to be a portrait painter thwarted by a need for increased financial security, Whale found a thriving market at major agricultural fairs for paintings of local landscapes, pictures of nature, and historical scenes. One of his most famous subjects is a panoramic view of Niagara Falls, often with a train in the foreground. So popular was the subject that Robert Whale duplicated it (with subtle differences) for a burgeoning market hungry to decorate their parlours with the majesty of "The Falls".

The painting depicts the suspension bridge crossing the gorge and the city of Niagara Falls, New York, in the distance. In the right foreground is an observation tower known as Street's Pagoda, a square 50-foot wooden tower built on Cedar Island by Samuel Street as a money-making scheme in the mid 1850s. The Pagoda was not a financial success due to its poor view of the Falls and eventually disappeared by the early 1900s along with Cedar Island itself — a casualty of progress as the narrow waterway to the mainland was filled in for construction of hydroelectric facilities.

Works by Robert Whale are in private and public collections including the National Gallery of Canada, Art Gallery of Ontario, Art Gallery of Hamilton, Sherbrooke Museum of Fine Arts, Montreal Museum of Fine Arts, and the McCord Museum in Montreal. Two of Whale's sons, John Claude Whale and Robert Heard Whale, as well as his nephew, John Hicks Whale, were also artists.

Oil on canvas, circa 1860, signed in the lower right corner R. Whale.

DRAUGHT HORSES

The carved horses, positioned as they are on each end of the fireplace mantle, appear as if they are about to step into the picture behind, becoming part of the scene, alert yet sure-footed as they steadily approach the majesty of Niagara Falls.

The quality of these horses is such that their beauty and power is instantly recognized, whether you're familiar with folk art and antiques or just a casual observer. Even though the maker's name has long been forgotten, the strength of the carvings speaks volumes.

The maker probably never thought of himself as an artist, just a farmer passing the time. The execution is simple, without any embellishment; however, instinct driven by a natural love of the horse has allowed the artist to capture not only the beauty of the animals, but their restrained power as well. Rather than a static stance, the horses are leaning slightly forward; one can feel the power in their chests and legs. The raised

legs, the head held high with chin tucked in, even the subtlety of the slight uphill angle of the terrain underfoot; all contribute to the artist's success in depicting his noble companions. Of particular interest are the different coloured bases (one green, one white); upon reflection this is an obvious reference to summer and winter, with the winter horse being just a bit heavier as they are with their winter coats; one can almost imagine the stones being hauled in the summer or the huge barrel of maple sap trailing behind on a sled in the snow-covered bush of late spring.

Carved in pine, each from a single block of wood, retaining the original brown paint over a red wash creating a chestnut colour on the body complemented by white and yellow paint for markings, harness, hooves, and eyes. Minor repairs undertaken with some restoration to tail and ears. Professionally mounted on a steel base for stability.

Ex: Ralph and Patricia Price collection.
Quebec, 19th century.

DIAMOND POINT ARMOIRE

It reaches out as you enter the room — this 18th century Quebec armoire with its faceted diamonds playing with the light in every direction. An iconic piece of Canadiana: elegant to some, sensual to others, impossible to ignore its presence.

In early Quebec furniture the relief carved diamond point panel evolved from the flat lozenge cut panel in the early 18th century and remained popular up to the 1825-30 period. The diamond relief is found on small buffets, interior doors, cradles, blanket chests, and armoires of all sizes. Occasional variations occur where multiple single diamonds adorn each panel, but typically the panels appear in either of two styles: they can be sculpted with a central diamond surrounded by four corner points or as a classic X-shaped St. Andrew's cross with a diamond in each quadrant. Frequently both styles will appear on the same door. The diamond motif can also still be seen as a painted design on barn doors throughout rural Quebec.

This large armoire is well balanced with diamond point panels not only on the doors but also on both sides. The central panels show a five-point diamond relief while the larger upper and lower panels each feature a sculpted St. Andrew's cross with its four faceted diamonds. Along with the prominent cornice and base moulding typical for the period, the doors are surrounded by a step moulding carved in the solid, not applied with nails or pegs as found in furniture of a later period. Interestingly, this architectural feature allows for the hinges to appear recessed, giving more emphasis to the diamond panels on the doors. The deep protruding diamonds are sharp and crisp, complemented beautifully by the original Prussian blue paint, original fiche hinges and hand-forged escutcheon.

When "picked", the armoire was in very good condition with the original feet intact, however, the original cornice and base moulding were missing; these mouldings have been carefully restored and colour matched to the original blue paint found on the case and doors. Restoration is a touchy subject for collectors, some preferring to leave things as found; however, sensitive restoration can be like preventive medicine, giving the piece back some pride and extending its lifespan for future generations. Seeking the guidance of fellow collectors and professionals should always be the first step.

Constructed in pine, with original shelves, natural unpainted interior, panelled hand-hewn back with pegged joints throughout, forged rose head nails affixing the top board, forged hinges, escutcheon, and the original lock and key.

Quebec, 1750-1775.

A VIEW OF DUNDAS — J. R. SEAVEY

Painted in 1884 from a viewpoint on the Niagara Escarpment overlooking Dundas, Ontario, this oil on canvas by Julian Ruggles Seavey (1857-1940) captures a changing time as a team of horses labours up the steep hill while a chugging train is seen on the left bank. The sleepy town rests below with Lake Ontario and a glimpse of Hamilton in the distance. Spencer Creek traverses the foreground. Identifiable landmarks include St. Augustine's Catholic Church in the centre and, just below, the original Methodist church (now St. Paul's United). To the right on the edge of Spencer Creek is the former Dundas Cotton Mill, out of business just a few years after Seavey recorded this scene and eventually demolished in 1973.

Of particular interest is the water leading away from the town — the Desjardins Canal built in 1837. Prior to the arrival of the railway, this dredged waterway through the marsh provided the Dundas region with important access to Lake Ontario and the port of Hamilton. In fact a large turning basin at Dundas

allowed large schooners to come and go with ease. By 1870 the canal traffic began to decline and, with the completion of a direct rail line to Dundas in 1895, the Desjardins Canal soon became a relic of the past.

Julian Ruggles Seavey arrived in Hamilton in 1879 after having studied art in New York, Paris, Rome, and Germany. He was a skilled artist capable of working in many different media but was best known for his still life pictures and landscapes. In 1897 a series of 95 drawings by Seavey, known as the Wentworth Landmarks, were published by the *Hamilton Spectator* depicting the churches, graveyards, inns, and mills of old Hamilton.

The hope was that the series would draw attention to these architectural gems as the city marched towards industrialization, changing the landscape forever. Today Seavey's works are coveted by local historians as a link to Hamilton's earlier times.

Seavey's career took a turn in 1908 when he joined the Hamilton Normal School to train public school teachers in art education. He remained there as head of the department until retirement in 1931. Seavey continued to lecture at the University of Toronto and became a strong advocate for the arts and the community of Hamilton in his later years.

Several works by Julian Ruggles Seavey reside in the Hamilton Art Gallery's permanent collection as well as in private collections.

DAMASE RICHARD

Being a farmer on the upper St. Lawrence was not an easy task in the 19th century and the winters were long and cold — the perfect climate for carving and whittling as a way to pass the time. For Damase Richard of Saint-Ubalde de Portneuf, this leisure time didn't come until his children could take over the daily chores of the farm in the late 19th century.

Born in 1852, Damase wasn't always a farmer, having first worked as a decorative painter for a carriage maker in Quebec City and in a furniture factory in Pont-Rouge. But in carving he found his niche, creating impressions of animals and birds primarily found on the farms and in the woods around him. A folk artist in the purest sense, his style was simple yet expressive in all the right places, a sense of unhurried passion as the creation developed in his hands with the simple tools at his disposal — two pocket knives, three gouges, a plane, and an axe. Without the means to acquire supplies, his carvings were also often intensely coloured in paint he reportedly mixed himself.

Nettie Sharpe is credited with the "discovery" of the Richard family after travelling the roads of Quebec in search of antiques and sculpture. Mrs. Sharpe was legendary as one of the first female "pickers" of

antiques in the 1950s, '60s, and '70s, knocking on doors and buying from other pickers and dealers, eventually amassing one of Canada's finest collections of early Quebec furniture, art, and folk carvings. As she did with Philippe Roy and others, she became a personal friend of Damase Richard's son Wilfrid who was following in his father's footsteps.

Damase Richard is one of the earliest "named" folk artists of rural Quebec. The carved and painted cat in this collection is an excellent example of the Richard style, with its deeply carved eyes, expressive features and smooth lines. From the alert expression in the face to the front legs carved into the chest and the tail wrapping around from behind, the cat takes on a lifelike quality as it surveys the room.

Damase was known to have given away his creations to friends and neighbours, or he would simply place his latest creation on a fence post at the end of his lane to be rescued by some passerby. But this cat was a family favourite, appearing several decades later with other carvings on a parade float assembled by son Wilfrid Richard as part of Saint-Ubalde's 100th anniversary celebration in 1960. This event may have been a catalyst for Wilfrid as he became a prolific folk artist in the mid to late 20th century selling his carvings to collectors and dealers alike.

Damase Richard was active from the late 19th century up to the 1920s, and died in 1922. His work is unsigned. Another black and white cat carved by Damase Richard — this one nicknamed *Le Harlequin* due to its painted black mask — is in the Canadian Museum of History as part of the Nettie Covey Sharpe collection bequest.

A carved squirrel by Damase Richard exhibiting the same strengths as the cat — simple yet expressive.

The carved songbird stands on wire legs on a black truncated base and is an excellent example of the strong colours often found on the bird carvings of Damase Richard.

NORTHWEST COAST MOTIF BLANKET CHEST

It takes a few minutes to appreciate the subtle motifs painted on this blanket chest, the colours blending perfectly with the tones in the room.

Originally "picked" by an Ontario student in the Hamilton area in the 1980s along with another box with similar decoration, the illustrated example passed through several hands before being offered at the Bowmanville Antiques and Folk Art Show* in April 2015. This box gives the appearance of an object created by a First Nations artist from Canada's spectacular Northwest Coast of British Columbia, however, it represents a bit of an enigma since it is more "folk" than traditional. It is constructed in pine, rather than cedar, and decorated in multiple colours instead of the more traditional red and black. Judging from the painting style it is highly likely that the decoration is the work of a non-Native in the late 19th or early 20th century.

Painted on all sides in red, blue, yellow, and black, the box has a thunderbird motif on the front and top with a raven and bear head on opposing ends, all common symbols of the Northwest Coast people such as the Haida and Tlingit.

The other decorated box collected at the same time is illustrated in *Canadian Folk Art to 1950*, page 404 and another, with Northwest Coast decoration on an early immigrant trunk, was recently sold at auction in France.

*The Bowmanville Antiques and Folk Art Show in Ontario, Canada, is a long-standing annual event that is known for early painted furniture, exceptional Canadian folk art from known and anonymous folk artists, and decorative accessories in a wide range of material; it is an instant education and visual experience for anyone who enters the hall.

CHAPTER 3

Library

Fitting with the nature of the room, the ambience in the library is "high country", decorated with casual comfort in mind but with a slightly more formal feel provided by the furniture produced in the early years of British settlement in eastern Canada. The more formal mood is, however, immediately softened with the floor-to-ceiling book shelves flanking a fireplace at the far end. Interspersing the books with strategically placed folk art also lightens the look and adds depth to the room.

The oval painting above the fireplace depicts a pivotal point in Canadian history recording the death of General Wolfe at Quebec, while also serving an important secondary function of hiding the television behind a hinged, easy-to-swing panel.

TIGER MAPLE CORNER CUPBOARD

Rooms with high ceilings can be difficult to decorate, breaking it up with a single large piece can be effective, whether it is a painting, furniture, or an architectural element.

Anchoring the library to the left of the entry is a tall glazed corner cupboard in figured maple and cherry from the Eastern Townships in Quebec; in the right corner is an Ira Twiss long-case clock in original grained surface, also from Quebec.

The simplicity of the corner cupboard is deceptive, as the clever use of the contrasting woods gives it an understated elegance that blends perfectly with the formal Maritime furniture elsewhere in the room. The use of cherry for the surround moulding and door frames complements the rich tone of the tiger maple primary wood. The surround moulding also frames the cupboard within the space, minimizing the scale somewhat. The alternating ladder arrangement of the mullions in the upper doors is unusual, as are the three drawers in tiger maple discreetly tucked away. The cupboard interior, with its original shelves, is overpainted in a matte off-white to soften the presence and provide an appropriate backdrop for the objects within.

Eastern Townships, Quebec, 1825-1840, excellent original condition including hardware and knobs.
Ex collection: George and Louise Richardson, Toronto.

1837 REBELLION BOX

It is easy to dismiss this tiny box with its finely inked script, but its place in Canada's history revolves around a story of passion, politics, alleged treason, and eventual death for some involved.

Rebellion boxes, like this one by William Alves, are also known as prisoner boxes or, morbidly, coffin boxes due to their shape and the perceived fate of their makers, all prisoners in the Toronto Jail awaiting trial for their role in the political rebellion of 1837 against the controlling power of the British in Upper Canada.

In early December 1837 a group of rebels led by William Lyon Mackenzie stormed down Toronto's Yonge Street on a mission to overthrow the government. Mackenzie had formidable credentials: newspaper publisher, former Member of Parliament, former mayor of Toronto, and a vocal political advocate for constitutional change.

Mackenzie and his men were forced to retreat, and two days later the authorities launched a devastating raid of Mackenzie's headquarters at Montgomery's Tavern. Mackenzie had chosen to launch the rebellion at that time because of a reduced local military presence due to local troops being deployed to Lower Canada to quell a similar uprising in Quebec led by Louis-Joseph Papineau.

William Alves was an idealistic 21-year-old employee at Montgomery's Tavern who was an ardent follower of Mackenzie and his cause; he was one of only 12 reformers sent to England for trial at the Old Bailey Courthouse in London. Alves was pardoned on condition that he not return to Canada and eventually settled in Ohio. Two of the organizers of the Rebellion were not so fortunate: Samuel Lount and Peter Matthews were hanged in Toronto in 1838. With a bounty on his head, William Lyon Mackenzie escaped prosecution by fleeing with other rebels to the United States; amnesty was decreed in 1849 and he returned home, eventually resuming a political career in Toronto.

According to *From Hands Now, Striving to be Free* (York Pioneer Society, 2009) this is one of two boxes completed by William Alves, the first one dated April 1838; the rebellion box in this collection was created after the young Alves had spent six months in jail, just prior to his trial in London, England. The top is inscribed *"A present to Miss Sophia Kelly, from William Alves, June 23, 1838"* while sides and bottom are inscribed with a poem inspired by Robert Burns. Was William a tentative suitor to Miss Kelly or was he just a friend?

Rebellion boxes are small (this one measuring 3.5" in length) and were made not only as a means to pass the time but also as a way for the rebels to express their feelings towards their cause and their loved ones. This box is typical, carved from a single piece of scrap wood with no joinery, and a sliding lid with a bevelled perimeter around a raised rectangular panel; the box is stained a reddish brown with lighter-colour, linen-fold panels on each side to accommodate the black script.

An interesting footnote to the story is that among the government forces in the attack on Montgomery's Tavern was 22-year-old John A. Macdonald, destined to become Canada's first prime minister in 1867. A few decades later the rebellion leader Mackenzie's grandson, William Lyon Mackenzie King, would take his first steps toward becoming the longest-serving prime minister of Canada.

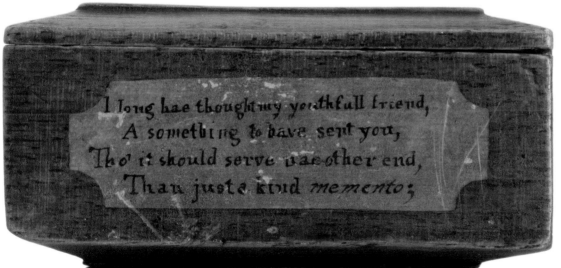

I long hae thought my youthfull friend,
A something to have sent you,
Tho' it should serve nae other end,
Than just a kind mementoe;

Oft clinging to the mossy grate,
  [perhaps the jail house door]
To catch a glimpse of heaven's pure light,
Uncertain as to future fate,
Yet hope in God to set all right;

The end of the poem is inscribed on the bottom of the box and unfortunately has worn away with time.

CARVED BRUSH

Every collection has a "what is it?" and this collection is no exception. Proudly displayed standing on a shelf in the tiger maple corner cupboard is an elongated brush, undoubtedly very old and made with care and skill, featuring carved motifs and a bristled hide neatly affixed with pegs to the wooden haft. It was likely made for a very specific purpose; however, research to date has proved fruitless in finding another example or information regarding its application.

Found in Quebec and carved in birch, the brush likely dates to the 18th century, judging from the carving style, shrinkage of the hide, patina of the wood, and the use of wooden pegs in lieu of iron brads. The style

and nature of the carving detail point to a Native origin: the tree motif on the back, the carved zigzag pattern in the centre, and especially the human head forming part of the pommel. The shape of the head and its facial details, especially the light moustache and beard, suggest an East Coast or subarctic tribe. Although facial hair was not the norm for indigenous people, early exposure to Europeans inevitably introduced different genetic characteristics. For example, several 19th century portraits in the collection of the Nova Scotia Museum show Mi'kmaq men with moustaches, beards, and even muttonchop sideburns.

The brush tapers to a point below the carved head with its wide-set eyes, the taper providing a perfect backdrop for the tree motif with branches reaching out from a centre spine, terminating with the trunk fading into a carved depression for the user's thumb. The coarse hair (likely elk or moose) also suggests the brush needed to be durable — not a brush for light work.

The Maliseet and Mi'kmaq both incorporated geometric eight-pointed stars and naturalistic designs into their clothing and tools. Painted and carved motifs were used for utilitarian objects from snowshoes and canoes to boxes, bowls, spoons, tools, and weapons. According to Chrestien LeClercq, a Franciscan Recollet who spent 12 years with the Mi'kmaq mission in 1675: "Indians believe in dreams and these dreams had to be acted out, made real, and sometimes incorporated as design work into personal possessions or clothing."*

LeClercq became a noted historian of Nouvelle France, publishing two major works in 1691 that included observations on Mi'kmaq lifestyle, customs, and beliefs.

The motifs on this brush, including the spiral carving on either side of the head, closely resemble carving found on early crooked knives made by the Mi'kmaq throughout eastern Canada. Aside from geometric circles found in quillwork, typical Mi'kmaq designs include loops, C-scrolls, zigzag motifs, and chevrons — virtually all of which are found on this brush.

Was it made for Native use or was it carved as a gift for a European contact? Is it of Northern origin, Mi'kmaq, or from another First Nations tribe in the St. Lawrence corridor? There are many questions, but without knowing its purpose they are even more difficult to answer. Speculation at best, the research continues.

Quebec, 1790-1820
Ex private collection, collected in Quebec by Nettie Sharpe.

*Glenbow Museum, *The Spirit Sings: Artistic Traditions of Canada's First Peoples* (McClelland and Stewart, 1987).

ABENAKI DEED BOXES

Displaying these carved and decorated deed boxes inside a corner cupboard is an unusual idea that proves to be very successful in showing the merits of each in its individual space while viewing the group as a whole. The impact is gradual as the eye moves from shelf to shelf taking in the similarities and differences of each piece. The boxes are somewhat naive in construction, likely made by a skilled yet self taught craftsman, and are decorated on the sides and dome tops with incised and painted foliage, hearts, diamonds, chevrons, and other geometric motifs.

The first two boxes, acquired at an antique show in Toronto in 2006, were originally found by Nettie Sharpe near Sainte-Angèle, a community (now part of Bécancour) on the south shore of the St. Lawrence River opposite Trois Rivières. The third box in the collection was acquired in 2013 through another antique dealer friend who recognized the similarities of construction, incised carving details, and paint colour — all factors that represent the "signature" of the unknown maker.

The naive construction details of hewn wood, pegs, and hand-cut dovetails could easily be the work of a habitant craftsman but, when combined with the rudimentary yet precise carving and the naturalistic details of motifs such as hearts, tree of life, chevrons, and vines, all signs point to a Native influence. This is supported by the knowledge that the region of Bécancour includes an Abenaki First Nations reserve that originated in the early 1700s as the Abenaki fled northern Maine following battles between New England and the Wabanaki Confederacy (specifically the Mi'kmaq, Maliseet, and Abenaki), who were allied with the French.

A fourth example of these carved and painted deed boxes is in the collection of the Canadian Museum of History as part of the Nettie Covey Sharpe bequest in 2002. How many more are out there? Perhaps there are other forms with the same finely incised symbols that might lead us to discovering the maker.

Deed boxes in birch, original incised carving and paint, pegged construction. Some of the boxes have later round nail reinforcements.
Quebec, 1820-1835.

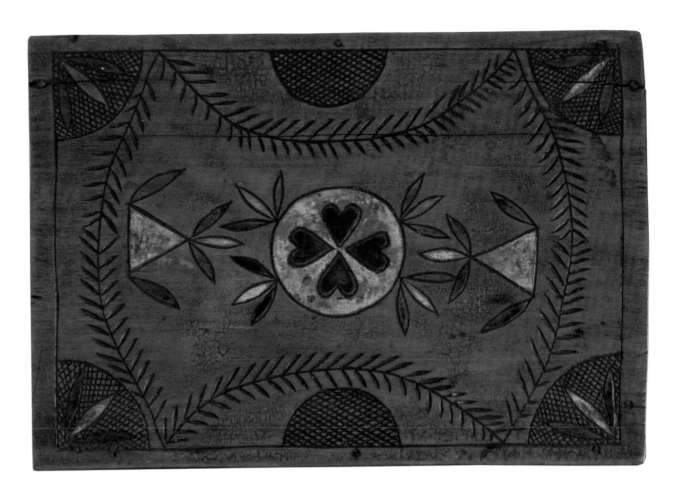

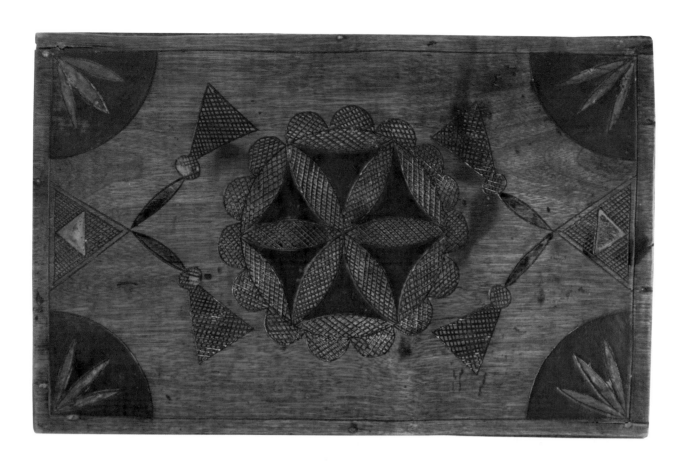

JOHN TULLES CARD TABLE

When asked to define antique Canadian furniture, the average response might be "primitive stuff" like a pine cupboard or farm table. Many Canadians would never consider that in the 18th and early 19th centuries, Canada's major centres in the Maritimes, Quebec, and Ontario produced formal mahogany furniture that was often on par with the best produced in England and the United States.

John Tulles of Halifax and Thomas Nisbet of Saint John are the two best known cabinetmakers in that category: beautiful mahogany tables, sofas, beds, chests, all manner of furniture of such high standards that some reside in American private collections and museums, mistakenly assumed to be of New England origin.

The Sheraton-inspired inlaid mahogany card table in the library is a superb example of this Maritime craftsmanship. Although the paper label has long disappeared, this fine table bears all the trademarks of John Tulles and closely resembles a labelled Tulles table now in a private collection. Although the labelled table has reeded legs rather than spiral rope-turned legs, both exhibit virtually identical form with canted corners to the skirt and top. Other shared classic Tulles signatures include the choice of light mahogany, the satinwood and ebonized string inlay around the skirt edge, the diamond inlays on the cut corners, and the fine dart-and-dot line inlay on the apron flanking a decorative inlaid square in the centre.

Interestingly, another example with the same rope-turned legs and the same inlay, but with rounded rather than canted corners, resides in the Royal Ontario Museum and has recently been attributed to John Tulles due to comparison with other known examples. The spiral rope turning is a nautical characteristic used by many English/Scottish cabinetmakers in the early 19th century to honour Nelson's victory against the French and Spanish naval forces at Trafalgar in 1805.

A feature of this form of card table is the flip top that is first rotated before opening the leaf, which then rests on the table frame, doubling the surface size and exposing the green baize-covered playing cloth. This action also reveals a hidden compartment where game pieces and cards would be kept.

John Tulles was born in Fife, Scotland, in 1771 and, according to research by Ross Fox, former curator of the Royal Ontario Museum in Decorative Arts, first appeared in Canada in 1806, where he worked as a house builder in Montreal. He had moved to Halifax by 1810 and started a cabinet-making business as a partner of Tulles, Pallister & McDonald — the firm was dissolved in early 1812 when the partners went their separate ways. It is fortunate that John Tulles used paper labels to identify some of his output, as it allows for authoritative attributions of certain pieces. Tulles died in Halifax in 1827.

An exquisite example of Canadian "high country" furniture. John Tulles, Halifax, Nova Scotia, circa 1820.

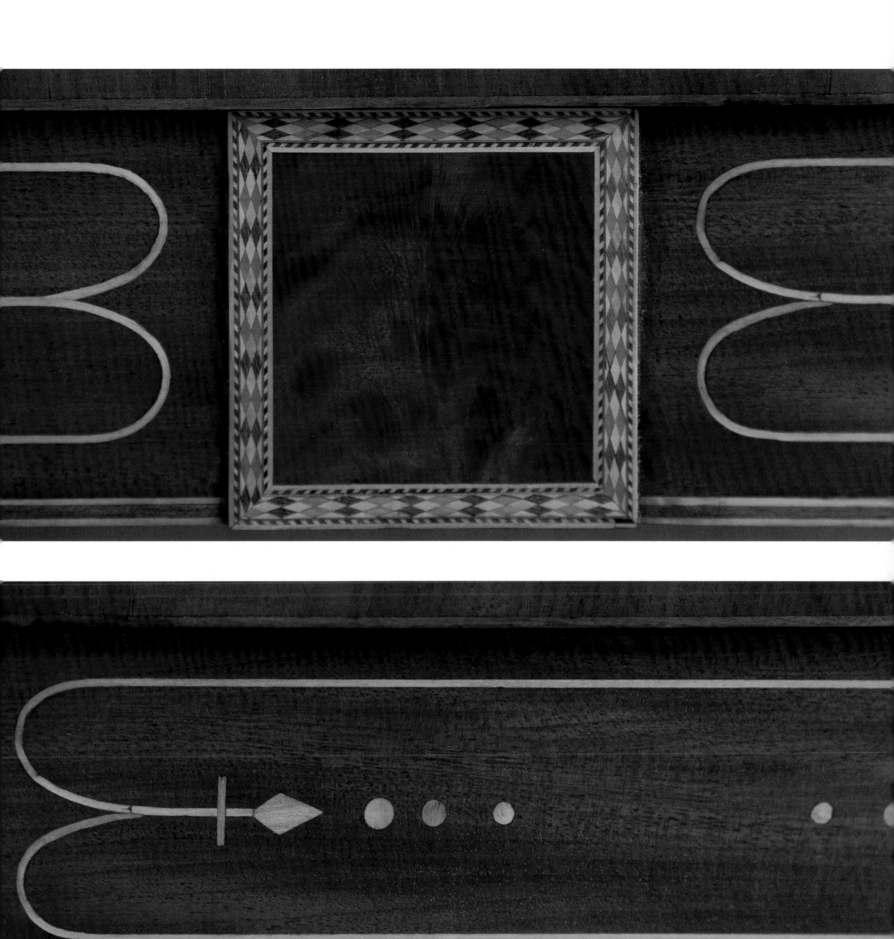

JOHN TULLES SIDE CHAIR

The Regency side chair sits quietly beside the tiger maple corner cupboard, its seemingly generic form concealing the artistry of the inlay patterns and applied mahogany rosettes.

Fashioned in birch with mahogany line and strip inlay, this chair is attributed as the work of Nova Scotia cabinet maker John Tulles due to the classic dart-and-dot mahogany inlay on the back crest that is similar in execution to the skirt detail on the card table discussed in the previous pages. Furthermore, the chair maker has added line inlay to the front seat rail and an unusually wide mahogany inlay (also found on Tulles table tops) up the front sabre leg and along the seat rail to the top of the back post. The single slat in the back features an inlaid rectangle supported by lyre-shaped extensions fitted to the back posts. Adding a sophisticated touch are the small mahogany rosettes applied to the top of the back posts as they curl behind the crest.

The top of the front rail of the chair bears the number XI, indicating it was one of a larger set, and an impressed mark *N. Anderson* in small letters. With no record of an N. Anderson working as a cabinet maker or wood worker in Nova Scotia at that time, it is most likely that the stamp represents the owner's name to avoid confusion with other large orders in the shop.

A masterful variation to a common form. Nova Scotia, attributed to the shop of John Tulles, Halifax, circa 1820.

HOLLAND LANDING RED MILL

This handcrafted and exquisitely painted model of the old red mill at Holland Landing, Ontario, now serves as a table centrepiece in the library. But it is a centrepiece with something to say — its function as an *objet d'art* is complemented by the history hidden within, laden with hopes and dreams, both dashed and realized.

The area known as Holland Landing (north of Toronto) was first discovered and mapped in 1791 by Samuel Holland, the first surveyor-general of British North America, acting under Governor John Graves Simcoe, who believed it would make an ideal shipping and defence point between York (now Toronto) and Georgian

Bay. The site was the northernmost point on the original alignment of Yonge Street, a major north-south route in Toronto today.

The mill was constructed in 1821 by Peter Robinson of Newmarket. A substantial structure, with quality workmanship and hand-planed boards inside and out, it was the only grist mill in the area and quickly became the hub of the growing village. Robinson was an enterprising individual and soon built a tavern on a lot close by. His talent for getting things done got the attention of the government and he was commissioned with overseeing the initial settlement of Peterborough in 1824. Three years later he was appointed surveyor-general of woods and forests for the province of Upper Canada and was also a member of the Legislative Council until his death in 1837. Although operated by an independent miller, Robinson still owned the Red Mill at that time.

This model was created by John Hill for his granddaughter just fifteen years after the mill's demise. It is meticulously crafted and painted in original red, green, and yellow, with an attention to detail that suggests an original structure that was well appointed indeed. How much is reality and how much is fantasy, we don't know, but the painted checkerboard floor, heart-shaped windmill blades, exceptional colours, and interior features all make this a significant piece of Canadian folk art.

It is extremely likely that the Red Mill was visited by at least two other historical figures: in 1825 Holland Landing marked the starting point for explorer Sir John Franklin's first overland trip to the Arctic Ocean, and Samuel Lount, an organizer of the 1837 Rebellion led by William Lyon Mackenzie, farmed and operated a blacksmith shop in the village. Lount was captured, convicted of treason, and hanged on April 12, 1838.

With modifications to steam power, the Red Mill operated into the late 19th century and then, after a few years of neglect, was razed by fire on March 2, 1894.

Ontario, early 20th century.

JEAN-BAPTISTE CÔTÉ — *L'HABITANT*

Unlike self-taught Quebec folk artists such as Damase Richard (1852-1922), Damase Rhéaume (1832-1903), or Phillipe Roy (1899-1982), Jean-Baptiste Côté (1834-1907) was a formally trained artist, making a living carving religious sculpture, figureheads, and trade signs. He was also an architect, wood engraver, carica-

turist, publisher, and printer, but today he is perhaps best known for his sculpture of animals of all description, meticulously hand-painted. Although some signed examples exist, much of his work was unsigned and it is certain that some of his figureheads and tobacco figures have found new homes over the years as Americana in the United States.

The *habitant* stands tall, simply attired in his khaki-coloured coat, brown tall boots, blue toque, and *ceinture fléchée* cinched tightly around his waist. His brush-like sideburns accentuate his square jaw and determined look. The hood of his coat descends in a deep V down his back, neatly bunched where the drawstring pulls through. There is no excessive carving, every fold is intended, every detail precise. This is not a caricature like many later carvings of this genre, this is a proud statement of the strength of the French-Canadian *habitant*.

Jean Baptiste Côté, along with his friend and eventual competitor Louis Jobin, learned his carving skills as an apprentice to François–Xavier Berlinguet, a highly regarded architect and sculptor who himself apprenticed to master Quebec sculptor Thomas Baillargé (1791-1859). This is just one example of how traditional academic 18th century carving skills continued in Quebec well into the 20th century.

In 1855 a young Jean-Baptiste Côté opened his first studio/workshop near the shipyards in Quebec's Lower Town and offered his services to the ship-builders — a booming industry at the time. By the early 1860s Côté had become more involved in Quebec politics, creating caricatures and political satire for *La Scie*, a political newspaper that understood the power of political cartoons and often aimed its sights at pro-Confederation Quebecers like George Etienne Cartier and Hector-Louis Langevin, or George Brown in Upper Canada.

The world changed for Côté by the 1870s prompting a change in his business model. With Confederation in place and his main customer base slipping away due to a slowly disappearing wooden shipbuilding industry, he began to accept a wider variety of commissions. Religious sculpture and tobacconist figures, trade signs, ink stands, and wall plaques, even magazine racks — by the 1880s Jean Baptiste Côté had emerged as one of Quebec's most popular carvers producing sculpture of all genres.

L'habitant, Jean-Baptiste Côté, Quebec, 1875-1880. A highly comparable signed example in a private collection supports this attribution.

NEW BRUNSWICK "NISBET" SEWING TABLE

Performing the task of supporting the *Habitant* sculpture by Jean-Baptiste Côté, this mahogany inlaid table is a masterpiece in its own right.

Very light in appearance, beautifully proportioned with a finely turned Sheraton leg, the three-drawer table is actually just two drawers — the lower deep drawer bearing two false fronts and likely used to store

sewing and knitting materials. After publishing *Heritage Furnishings of Atlantic Canada*, Henry Dobson had some second thoughts about this table — although described as being from Halifax, Nova Scotia, 1810-1815, the table's features started to look more and more like the work of Thomas Nisbet who was active at the same time in Saint John, New Brunswick (see the discussion on the Nisbet Legislative Desk, page 154, for more background on Thomas Nisbet).

Constructed in dark mahogany with white pine as the secondary wood, the table is in excellent original condition with its original locks and brass escutcheons. The brass pulls were switched to wooden knobs many years ago. The edge of the top incorporates a triple bead, a feature common with many Nisbet tables, the leg turnings are in the Nisbet style with ring turnings on the shaft and the rings originally ebonized, again typical of Nisbet. The brass cup casters are original and typical. The leg turning is virtually identical to two other tables now attributed by some connoisseurs as being Nisbet, one illustrated as plate 127 in *A Provincial Elegance*, which significantly appears to have the same diagonal band inlay of alternating light and dark strips found on the drawer fronts of the table in this collection; the other example with a similar leg is in *Heritage Furnishings of Atlantic Canada* illustrated as plate 104.

This table is an excellent example of the high quality furniture that was produced by skilled artisans in Canada long before Confederation.

New Brunswick, circa 1820. Attributed to Thomas Nisbet, Saint John, New Brunswick.

BIRD SCULPTURES — JEAN-BAPTISTE CÔTÉ

Throughout his career as a master sculptor, Jean-Baptiste Côté (see discussion of the *Habitant* sculpture on page 84) was also a whittler in his spare time, always with a pocket-knife in hand according to some reports. He was an especially prolific carver of animals and birds, some which he would leave behind after visits with friends.

This small carved rooster is an excellent example of his early period, with exacting attention to form and detail as well as superb paint and fine brush strokes. The cockerel is perfectly balanced and proud as he sits on a carved Quebec shelf in original robin's egg blue paint, cleverly mounted within one of the library bookcase compartments. This interruption of the book pattern adds interest and also highlights the importance of the small sculpture that may otherwise be lost in an open space.

Like this rooster, the early bird carvings by Jean-Baptiste Côté generally have heavy wire legs, mounted on a simple wooden base. Another recurring signature in all these birds and others seen by the author is a distinctive slightly flattened body shape. Although certainly not unique to Côté alone, when the flattened style is combined with excellent stylized paint, wire legs, subtle yet distinctive wing profile, simple unembellished form, and appropriate age and quality, then it is reasonable to suggest Jean-Baptiste Côté as the possible carver. Three other birds in the collection carved at least 20 years later — a cardinal, a blue jay, and a parrot — are attributed to Jean-Baptiste Côté on the basis of these signature characteristics.

The missing link that supports this conclusion is found at the Canadian Museum of History, where a carving of a *Parrot on a Speckled Roost* is identified as a sculpture by Jean-Baptiste Côté (Nettie Covey Sharpe collection). The Museum bird features the exceptional paint and decoration found on the earlier Côté rooster illustrated here, but with similar body form and size as the later blue jay, cardinal, and parrot. The *Parrot on a Speckled Roost* was included along with other notable bird carvings in an exhibition at the McCord Museum in Montreal in 1976 entitled *La volière enchantée* ("The Enchanted Aviary") published in *Vie des Arts*, vol. 20, no. 82. Other birds by Jean-Baptiste Côté were also on display.

Adding further credence to the theory is that the red cardinal in the collection was purchased by the author directly from collector/dealer Nettie Sharpe who claimed it to be the work of Côté, likely done in his retirement years on île d'Orléans in the early 1900s. By the time these birds with the twisted wire legs

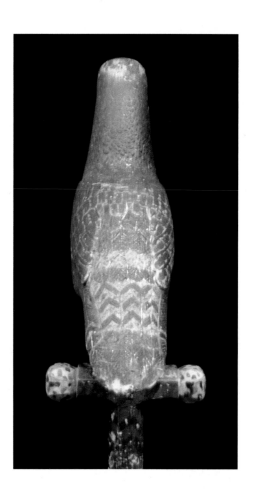

were made, Côté was approaching old age, his fingers not as nimble and the eyes a little weaker, but upon close examination the style evolution is apparent.

These three later carvings share the same body shape with raised wing profile as the illustrated rooster and the museum's parrot. Stylistic similarities in the original painted surface of the rooster, the museum parrot, and the red cardinal in the collection are evident. Naturally the paint on the later bird is more simplified yet the attention to style, colour, and detail remains. Due to this evidence it appears that the three birds with the twisted heavy wire legs share the same lineage as the small rooster profiled in this discussion and the Canadian Museum of History's *Parrot on a Speckled Roost* — all carved by Jean-Baptiste Côté, albeit at different points in his career.

Jean-Baptiste Côté and his friend and competitor Louis Jobin were among the last of the academically trained sculptors working in Quebec at the dawn of the 20th century. In their day they both created exceptional religious and secular works that are now found in situ or in public and private collections. By 1903 the health of Jean-Baptiste had begun to decline and after years of being at the top of his field, he died in poverty in Quebec City in 1907.

Parrot on a Speckled Roost,
Jean-Baptiste Côté
Canadian Museum of
History, 2002.125.980,
S2003-4554. Bequest
of the Nettie Covey
Sharpe Estate.

STEVENS FAMILY PORTRAITS

Canadian family portraits that pre-date 1850 are rare on the marketplace, primarily a result of a significantly smaller population base and fewer itinerant artists compared to those in New England during that time period.

 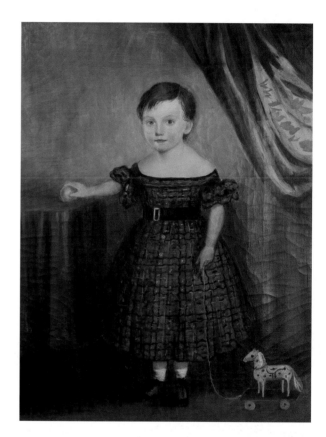

These three oil-on-canvas portraits descended through the New Brunswick Stevens family, former United Empire Loyalists, and were painted in the 1840-50 period judging by the costume and furnishings visible in the pictures. As a UEL family they likely arrived in New Brunswick by the end of the 18th century, suggesting that the portraits of the father and his two children were painted in this country. The whereabouts of the mother is unknown.

New Brunswick, circa 1845, artist unknown.

NEWFOUNDLAND KEEPSAKE BOX

Much like the impact resistant covers we use to protect our high-tech phones today, carved wooden containers were used by 19th century travellers, from clergy to sailors, to protect their books and keepsakes.

Generically known as bible boxes because they were often made to protect prayer books or small bibles from rough pioneer life, the term ditty box is often heard in the Maritimes for small boxes used by sailors and soldiers to store sewing materials and keepsakes to keep things safe and dry. In the lumber camps smaller book-like boxes were also made and are known as spruce gum boxes, their purpose self-evident. In all cases these boxes are typically carved from one piece of wood, hollowed out inside, decorated with a variety of religious or secular symbols, and affixed with a sliding end to access the contents. Larger examples are often constructed with hinges to minimize wear and tear on what is stored inside.

This particular box from Colliers, Newfoundland, is an exceptional example of naive art, possibly made by a sailor to store his mementos while away from home. Painted in three colours, it is elaborately decorated with one side exhibiting two abstract diamonds incised within a larger rectangle.

On the other side is a mini game board in yellow and black along with a crude two-colour swirling "good luck" symbol within an incised zigzag red border. The 64-square checkerboard is not just decoration; it would certainly have been used in leisure times with small playing pieces stored inside. Predominantly featured in the design is a bold red heart incised within a polygon centre symbol. The overall image is compelling, like a Picasso painting, so abstract yet purposeful.

Colliers, Newfoundland, circa 1810.

DEATH OF WOLFE

The far wall of the library features large open shelves on each side of a centred fireplace with wall panelling above — the perfect frame for a painting such as this one depicting the death of Wolfe. But what we don't see is even more important — the television discreetly hidden behind the hinged wall panel with the painting firmly affixed.

Many interpretations of Benjamin West's famous 1770 painting of the battlefield death of General Wolfe were made in the late 18th century as Wolfe's popularity and the significance of the British victory at Quebec became more apparent. This provincial rendition dates from the early 19th century and is painted in the oval, purchased as an architectural cartouche, but it could also have been the bottom of a tin tray. The scene is quite true to West's original, which in itself is a romantic interpretation of Wolfe's death on the battlefield with all his aides, soldiers, and a Native warrior looking on.

Major General James Wolfe was killed at the Plains of Abraham while leading British forces in their conquest of Quebec City on September 13, 1759. This marked the turning point in the Seven Years War that soon resulted in the end of French rule in North America. Wolfe's French counterpart in the battle, the Marquis de Montcalm, also died on the field of battle that day.

McGEE TABLE

When you look at this table you really get the meaning of "flame birch", as the lower drawer seems to be on fire with the dramatic figure in the wood. Attributed to a Mr. McGee whose workshop was located on the outskirts of the village of Berwick, Nova Scotia, it is in untouched condition retaining its original knobs and a nicely crackled varnish surface.

The table is constructed entirely in birch with a predominant flame pattern visible on virtually every surface, so strong that it almost hides the mahogany string inlay found on the drawer fronts, leg posts, and both perimeter and edge of the top. In true Nova Scotia style, the line inlay on the drawer fronts is interrupted in each corner by a dime-size dot and the same naive line-and-dot inlay appears just above the turnings on the front legs. The turnings are clean and efficient, striking the right balance for a table of this dimension.

This line-and-dot inlay is frequently found on both formal and country furniture in early Nova Scotia settlements while the squat form is not unusual for the Maritimes and gives the table substantial presence in a room. The two deep drawers provide ample storage for modern lifestyles.

Little else is known of Mr. McGee, who died in 1870, although his tool box and other furniture pieces are rumoured to exist in a private collection in the Maritimes and another table attributed to him is illustrated as plate 123 in *Heritage Furnishings of Atlantic Canada* by Henry and Barbara Dobson.

Nova Scotia, Kentville area, circa 1830.

❧

CHAPTER 4

Dining Room/Kitchen

T he strategic positioning of furniture, folk art, and floor coverings successfully divides the space in the common room into three distinct areas: living room, dining area, and kitchen.

In the dining room a candle, turned and carved, three-tier chandelier is the focal point hanging over a ten-foot contemporary cherry oval table. A carving of Napoleon sets a serious tone at one end of the table, while at the other end is a whimsical trade sign from a Quebec City fruit and vegetable vendor.

The kitchen workspace remains highly functional but features a tavern trade sign hanging overhead and folk art judiciously placed in the window and on the granite countertop.

THE HURON BOX

The painted oval box dazzles on the Nova Scotia mahogany card table as the morning sunlight bounces off the contours of its carved top. It draws you in, begging you to pick it up and admire its beauty.

Beautiful in form and colour, this object is identified as the "Huron Box" in published literature and has an unusually high-profile dome top with deeply carved geometric motifs. Decorated in three colours (black, red, and yellow), the cover motif builds in three sections: a lower oval band with deep chip carving surrounds the perimeter, next is an oval fringe of vertical carved ridges encircling the centre feature of chip carving, with eight linked rings forming rounded hearts. At the centre is a carved five-pointed star. The lap joints of both the cover and the box have an unusual undulating profile and are tightly stitched together.

The Huron Box is one of many of indigenous origin with gouge carving and geometric symbols (including flat-top painted and carved Mi'kmaq examples), but the design is more rudimentary in execution than others in the collection where a more refined Friesian style carving is found (see Convent Boxes, page 114). This latter style is characterised by extremely complex arrangements of finely carved geometric designs incorporating pinwheels, stars, triangles, and circles.

Oval banded boxes are all typically humble in their construction, with pegged or nailed pine bottoms, very thin sidewalls, and a plain unadorned wide band around the cover. The walls and perimeter band of the tops are typically stitched at the seams using spruce root or twine, while other examples feature overlapping finger joints or small iron brads to affix the lap. The majority of these oval boxes have a slightly domed cover with incised details or chip carving.

Ex collection Musée de l'Hôtel Dieu, Quebec, Canada.
Illustrated *Pleasing the Spirits*, Douglas C. Ewing, 1982.
Exhibited Metropolitan Museum of Art, New York, 1983.
Ex Sotheby's New York auction of the Herbert G. Wellington collection.

CONVENT BOXES

As explained in the previous discussion of the Huron Box, there are many superbly carved oval boxes crafted by First Nations people in addition to sculpted cradle boards, weapons, and domestic tools. There are many other oval boxes, however, that were long thought to be of Native origin but upon closer study suggest the influence of a European hand, exhibiting a level of quality in the design and carving that speaks of a sophisticated, trained skill set.

Many of these boxes were found and assumed made on the north shore of the St. Lawrence between Trois Rivières and Quebec City at a time when the Catholic Church was instrumental in the development of the new colony, as noted in *Folk Art — Primitive and Naive Art in Canada* by Blake McKendry. In fact the first two religious orders in Canada were established in 1639 in Quebec City with the arrival of the Ursuline nuns, who took it upon themselves to educate and "civilize" the Native girls, while the Hospitaliers de l'Hôtel Dieu concentrated on providing health care for the local and indigenous population.

Huron, Algonquin, and Iroquois children were all involved in the education program, according to historian Marius Barbeau. The curriculum included French manners, housekeeping, needlework, drawing, painting, music, some notions of architecture, and other fine arts. However, as Barbeau says in his foreword to *The Arts of French Canada (1630-1870)*, once the community began to prosper the nuns had to look to other activities to support their missions: "Several minor crafts also provided the nuns with a much needed income ... for instance the making of birch-bark boxes and dishes, fine leather work, book binding.... The making of birch-bark and incense boxes became, for the Ursuline as for other nuns in Quebec, especially remunerative." Barbeau explains further that the nuns then focused on the education of young French Canadian girls, going beyond exceptional embroidery skills to more practical skills such as gilding, painting, and even carving. Many of the skills for the above crafts might have been learned by the nuns from their indigenous students. Furthermore, although geometric symbols are common to all cultures, the inspiration for these motifs on the carved oval boxes may have come from early missionary contact with the Mi'kmaq who, according to Ruth Whitehead in *Micmac Quillwork,* were incorporating eight-pointed stars and assorted geometrics in their porcupine quill decorated bark boxes as early as the mid-18th century.

An example in this collection supporting the link between these carved oval boxes and religious Orders is a large black painted box with four wooden wheels on the underside. The carving on this box is Friesian in nature (see discussion on Huron Box) with a large swirling pinwheel on the top surrounded by gouge carved triangles painted white on the black ground. A zigzag chip carved border surrounds the base while a scalloped and carved apron adorns the oval band of the top. Below this is a medial moulding encircling the box, but most unusual are the four original wooden wheels pegged to the base. It is unlikely that wheels would have been part of a Native-inspired design in the 18th century. The design suggests that the contents of the box were intended to be shared with others — perhaps it contained different coloured threads and was passed from nun to nun across the convent work table as they created the elaborate needlework specimens found in some Quebec churches, museums, and private collections today?

Another recently acquired carved oval box exhibits the same fine geometric carving on the dome top but with a long incised floral vine that terminates in a stylized flower pot — again not a common design of an 18th century indigenous carver. Pertinent to this discussion are several oval boxes bearing a French name and often a late 18th century date inscribed on the bottom such as the one illustrated as plate 211 in McKendry's *Folk Art*, written on the bottom "Reine S … Marsière 1773". Was this the owner or the maker? If it was only marked for identification purposes then there is less of a reason to include the date; if it was a gift then the date would likely be more specific as to month and day; if it were the signature of the maker then the year of its creation was a logical inclusion.

To conclude, in addition to the superb Native carved examples such as the Huron Box and the flat-top style produced by the Mi'kmaq, the evidence strongly suggests that these domed oval boxes with finely executed Friesian style carving were either a co-operative effort of the Ursuline and Native population or the independent work of the nuns and schoolgirls taught by the religious orders of New France during the late 18th century.

Mi'kmaq box

SEMINARY PARROT

It may seem strange that exotic animals like lions, giraffes, and parrots are often represented in Canadian folk art and also appear on early transfer print tableware made for the Canadian market in the 19th century. In some cases it was in reference to historical symbols or religious stories, while in others it is a pure flight of fancy based on literature or reports from mariners returned from distant lands.

This carved parrot in the collection is a great example of pure folk art fancy. With a mate illustrated on the cover of the 1979 catalogue for the Bowmanville Antiques and Folk Art Show, the carved and decorated hanging parrot is one of a reported 24 bird-hoop carvings found suspended from a tree on the grounds of a Quebec seminary. Mounted in a hoop that may have been a small wagon rim, the parrot is bold yet simply carved with an oversize body that dominates the ring as he extends up and out for a view. Created in the early 20th century, the parrot is carved in pine, painted in bold enamel paint, and, as with the other known examples, has shaped feet carefully fabricated in tin. In true folk art fashion, the hoops in all cases appear to be made from whatever oval or round metal form was available at the time.

Offered at the Bowmanville Show in 1993, this parrot escaped Canada after being purchased by an American couple with a keen eye for the best. Almost 20 years later, with the help of a nudge from a mutual friend, the American collectors agreed to let the bird fly home in 2005 to roost in the Burneys' kitchen window. Aside from the daily joy of seeing the parrot in the window, the added pleasure is in knowing that a piece of Canadian history has returned. In recent years many significant and iconic objects have been repatriated by astute collectors across Canada who are united by a common passion to seek out and preserve our best material heritage whenever possible.

This parrot is illustrated as the first item in the catalogue for the 20th anniversary of the Bowmanville Antiques and Folk Art Show, directly opposite a photo of the other parrot from 1979. A third example from the original group, again with hoop and a commanding parrot, is illustrated in a room setting on page 165 in *The Painted Furniture of French Canada* by John A. Fleming.

THREE-TIER CHANDELIER

Repatriated from the United States in 2008, this three-tiered, carved chandelier is a Canadian classic that originally would have been one of several lighting the vast interior of a Catholic church in Quebec. Today, with its 28 candles lit, this exquisite sculpture hangs over the dining room table and fills the space with a warm glow, flickering on the various pieces of art and furniture around the perimeter.

Turned and carved chandeliers have been documented in Quebec since the early 18th century and were crafted for large homes or churches by some of the great sculptors of the day, including François Baillairgé, François-Xavier Berlinguet, Louis Quévillon, André Achim, and others, as noted in *The Early Furniture of French Canada* by Jean Palardy. They were produced in single, double, and, rarely, three tiers, sometimes boasting as many as 38 candles each.

This chandelier dates from the early 19th century and is marked with the number "10", identifying it as one of several for the church records. It is created in a restrained Louis XIV style incorporating foliate carving on the turned central shaft, which is divided into three vase-shaped sections: the upper and lower sections are carved with acanthus leaves on the bowl while the central vase features scalloped lobes; the neck of each vase is gouge carved with vertically tapering lobes terminating in a black ring. The arms are shaped from iron rods with carved balls at mid-point, terminating in turned and painted candle sockets. An unusual feature of this chandelier is the presence of curved iron hooks that encircle each vase at mid-point — perhaps to temporarily hang candles while cleaning out the wax residue in the sockets.

The contrasting black and gold paint is commonly found on chandeliers of this period (often a dark green substitutes the black) and is highly effective in highlighting the sculptural details thereby increasing the visual power and beauty of the object. When all candles are lit, the illumination and ambience are remarkable and virtually impossible to duplicate with modern light.

Quebec, 1825-1840.

S.J. DOYLE/J.A. MAHAR TRADE SIGN

"Two countries — one heart" was the slogan in 2001 of a festival celebrated by border neighbours St. Stephen, New Brunswick, and Calais, Maine. The same sentiment existed at the times when S.J. Doyle and J.A. Mahar separately operated the public room in the community International Hotel.

Tavern signs from the 19th century are a rarity — most were destroyed once their usefulness had expired or the building was torn down. Most signs simply advertise the inn without much embellishment; some, like this one, show in graphic detail what kind of solace one might find inside. The images on the sign tell us unequivocally that the International Hotel was a place where friends from both sides of the border would meet to share some gossip and a cold beverage.

According to local historians, the towns of St. Stephen and Calais were thought of as one community 150 years ago, with a border in between. People like S.J. Doyle and J.A. Mahar lived in New Brunswick but worked every day in Maine. The spirit of co-operation is evident with the two flags (Stars and Stripes and a Canadian Red Ensign) equally draped on either side of the oval central image that shows shelves of coloured bottles and the raising of glasses in friendship as two hands reach over the bar.

Incredibly, all these elements had been hidden under layers of black paint and grime; just as in an archaeological dig, this dark overcoat was carefully removed. Inch by inch the images appeared — first the flags were exposed and then the bottles on the shelf came to life, one by one. At one point in the hotel's lifespan the ownership changed as the name J.A. Mahar was lettered in gold block type over the original S.J. Doyle. Both S.J. Doyle and J.A. Mahar are buried in St. Stephen, New Brunswick.

Double sided so it likely hung over the boardwalk in front of the hotel, same image both sides, original paint, descending directly from the family of J.A. Mahar in New Brunswick. This trade sign dates from the 1875 period; the International Hotel was built some time after the American Civil War in Calais, Maine, and was gone by the late 1890s.

CARVED FIGURE OF NAPOLEON

From a decor point-of-view, a small cupboard against a high wall can be problematic. A large painting or textile above the cupboard could be overpowering, in this case diminishing an important piece, while a group of objects or a single weathervane would not be enough to occupy the blank space. This exceptional pine carving of Napoleon is a successful choice that complements the small cupboard on many levels: the faux white marble colour of the sculpture harmonizes beautifully with the pastel blue cupboard and its white highlights; the scale of the sculpture is ideal for filling the vertical space while not smothering the cupboard below; and, of course, the classic French lines of the armoire are complemented at an intellectual level with the romantic image of the former French emperor.

Napoleon seems to be content with his view. Arms crossed, head high, this almost life-size pine sculpture captures the essence of the man as a strategic warrior and leader of the French people through the first quarter of the 19th century. Although Napoleon was a threat to the British Empire, his military acumen was admired and studied by friend and foe alike, and the Napoleonic code became the foundation for the governing principles of modern countries around the world.

This sculpture was found in Granville Ferry, New Brunswick, where it had resided for many years in the Troop family homestead. The Troop family operated a line of some 60 sailing vessels at their peak and were key figures during the Golden Age of Sail where New Brunswick timber used for ship building was transported to England during the Napoleonic wars. The figure bears the signs of a schooled carver who likely worked in the trade fashioning figureheads and other trade or religious sculpture. Possible sculptors include Edward Charters (1801-1882) of Saint John, who carved a stern board of Marco Polo in 1851 for one of the largest ships to be built in New Brunswick. Notably, Charters also trained his nephew John Rogerson, who worked in New Brunswick and Boston in the late 19th century and became renowned as a sculptor of high quality figureheads, tobacconist figures, and trade signs.

Another similar size carving of Napoleon (ex: Harbinson collection) is now in the collection of the Canadian Museum of History, attributed to Michael Grace of Sackville, New Brunswick.

As-found condition, old white overpaint over original faux marble surface, age cracks, no repairs or restoration.
New Brunswick, 19th century.

LOUIS XV ARMOIRE

Elegant and sophisticated, feminine yet strong, the size, colour, carving, and detail of this 18th century small armoire all contribute to its status as a fine example of early Quebec furniture.

Illustrated in its entirety with Napoleon in the previous discussion, the French manner of construction is found with pegged joints, integral carved mouldings in the door frame rails and stiles, pin and barrel hinges, panelled back, and original shelves. It also has the rare feature of a removable cornice, a development that was generally reserved for larger, more imposing cupboards, designed to facilitate moving the armoire without damaging the crown. Sometimes it is only the cornice moulding that is removable; in other cases, such as with this armoire, the cornice comes off complete with the top boards, in one piece. When the lift-off doors are also removed it then becomes a simple matter to move the armoire from room to room or pop out the joinery pegs and transport the cupboard in pieces.

It is rare to find the removable cornice intact; naturally, since the cornice is removable, many armoires got separated from their "hats" (as in the case of the diamond point armoire in this collection), with the cornice being misplaced or destroyed as the armoire eventually found itself relegated to lesser status over its 250 year history.

Also setting this armoire apart from the standard Louis XV form is the complexity of the upper door panel and the wide and deeply carved surround moulding. Rather than the standard rectangular panel with a single carved volute on the top edge, this armoire features a carved double volute spiral surmounted by the relief carved double sprig of flowers highlighted in white paint over the original French blue. This latter effect provides a fresh and invigorated look and is in concert with the Louis XIV/XV style where natural elements are occasionally employed such as flowers, vines, shells, and other ornamentation derived from nature. The carved floral "burst" at the top of the panel is certainly not an afterthought as the stem of the branch seems to magically grow out of the ascending and descending curves.

The classic S-curves of the Louis XV form are found on the top rail of the upper panel, while the lower rail with its symmetrical deeply cut moulding is more Louis XIV in inspiration. The sharp upper tip of the lower edge moulding is reflected in the sharply defined raised panel, almost drawing your eyes upwards to the floral motif. The careful matching of the shape of the raised panel to the flowing lines of the frame contributes to the power of the design. The cornice with its dentil motif is a feature generally associated with the Adam period, which in Canada typically dates to the first quarter of the 19th century; however, in the broader view this is a Neoclassic influence that is also found on Quebec armoires dating from the very early 18th century. In this armoire, the cornice features stepped details (not the Ogee style of later Adam cupboards) that, when combined with the early feature of removability and the other construction features as noted above, suggest an 18th century date for this cupboard.

This armoire was discovered in a back shed in Montreal, over-painted but amazingly intact with its full height and original cornice, shelves, and doors. The brown overpaint was carefully removed to reveal the exceptional pale blue and white. Minor edge repair to one side of cornice.

Quebec, 1760-1775.

FRUIT VENDOR TRADE SIGN

Trade signs appear in many forms and in all types of materials; some are simply flat boards with a painted message, some are two-sided, and others, like cigar store figures, can be found in three-dimensional form.

This fruit vendor trade sign used by a Quebec City merchant at the turn of the 20th century is an interesting example, carved and decorated on both sides. It is designed to accommodate a support bracket underneath so it could hang over the sidewalk as pedestrians ambled by. Today it makes a unique statement as a decorative table centrepiece or sculpture on a sideboard.

The lattice work of the basket is relief carved in a plank of wood, while the fruit are individually carved and applied to the basket. Taking into consideration the original viewing angle from the sidewalk below, the sign creator has remembered to enlarge the fruit slightly so the size looks natural from the street level, and has carved them in full form to give the impression that the produce is almost tumbling out of the basket.

In original paint, with minor touch-ups, this is a rare Canadian trade sign.

Quebec City, circa 1900.

FORT DUQUESNE GAME BOARD

Game boards are generally valued by collectors for the graphic appeal of their patterns and colours. This example from the collection is no exception, but it also has the merit of age, 1821 being extremely early for a North American game board. The board is also unusual due to it being an "asalto" game of military strategy instead of the typical checkers or Parcheesi boards readily available on the market today.

Purchased as a Quebec game board due to the presence of both French and British flags and the bold title *Jeu d'Assaut* (Assault Game) along the bottom edge, a little research and deductive reasoning reveal a deeper story. The decoration actually depicts the defeat of a distant French fort near what is now Pittsburgh, Pennsylvania, at a time when the countries of Canada and the United States as we know them today weren't even on the map.

The design is striking with its white lines and red dots on an alternating dark blue or green ground complemented by intricately painted images of cannons, stacked cannon balls, military tents, forts, and

flags. The stonework of the fort is well defined with crenellations around the edge of the wall and two gold-painted guard houses at the entrance to the fort. Beside the title in smaller print are the initials A.M. (presumably the maker) accompanied by the inscription *Pitt 10th Feb. 1821*.

Given the military imagery, Pitt assuredly refers to Fort Pitt, formerly Fort Duquesne in the French Régime period that was destroyed by the British in 1758 and re-constructed as Fort Pitt in honour of William Pitt the Elder, British secretary of state. Fort Pitt would become Pittsburgh in 1816. Further supporting the Fort Duquesne attribution is that the fortifications on the board are showing the French flag while the tents around the fort show the British Ensign — a flag used by Britain in its colonies in the 18th century. It is clear from the imagery with the cannons spewing smoke that the French fort is under attack. Also linking the game board to this area is the style of cannon depicted — in 1804 a foundry was established nearby to manufacture cannons and cannonballs. In 1821, coincidentally the date on the game board, a new cannon was produced at the factory with a very distinctive slender design, just like the long slender cannons depicted on the board.

Most game boards on the market today date from 1870-1930; this board is a particularly rare example, not only initialled and dated 1821 but with superb graphics and history as well. So who was the maker A.M.? Could they be the initials of a descendant of a French soldier who fought at Fort Duquesne during the Seven Years War between the French and English for control of North America?

We'll never know but it's always fun to wonder.

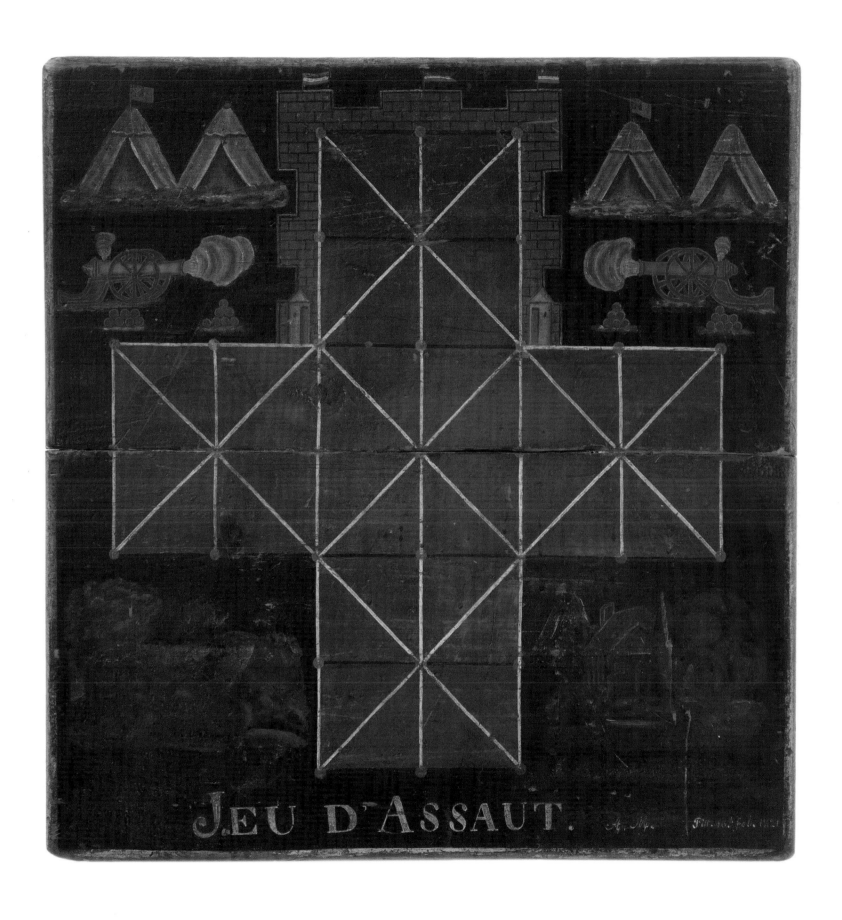

JEU D'ASSAUT.

CHAPTER 5

Bedrooms/Bathrooms

Hooked rugs are found in all the bedrooms and bathrooms of the house, frequently placed on larger sisal mats to protect the hooked rug from sliding on the floor and getting damaged. Some rugs are wall mounted as tapestries, while weathervanes and folk art complete the goal of creating a relaxed environment for every one of these rooms.

HOOKED RUG — LAURENTIAN VILLAGE

It is better than most window views — a massive hooked rug in the master bedroom with a dramatic Quebec Laurentian winter scene copied from a 1920s painting by noted Quebec painter Clarence Gagnon (1881-1942). Repatriated from the United States after being seen in show coverage in an American trade journal, the rug now graces the wall in the master bedroom with its magnificent colours and dramatic composition.

Clarence Gagnon was a passionate supporter of the arts and crafts of the Charlevoix region and assisted local rug hookers in creating designs and plans for their projects. His desire was to re-establish Quebec as a source of quality handicraft objects and folk art.

Gagnon is known to have conceptualized and fabricated the frames for many of his early works. At his first major exhibition held in Paris in 1913, Gagnon had some 80 works on display with 54 being Quebec scenes, all of which were displayed in frames painted and decorated by the artist himself. Typically the frames would be a dark background with floral/fauna or geometric designs along the edge.

This hooked rug seems to duplicate that effort in creating a frame that becomes one with the scene, uniting the two as a single piece of art. The inner "mat" and mouldings are simulated by the use of different coloured strips framing the picture and then the "frame" itself replicating Gagnon's early framing technique of coloured decoration on a black background.

Just as Gagnon likely took some artistic license in creating the original painting, so did the rug hooker in adding a green picket fence to the scene as well as enlarging and changing the colour of the house in the foreground and adding four large windows, the bottom two with flower pots displayed. The snow is fresh and the air is crisp with wisps of smoke coming from the chimneys as a single sleigh and walker brave the chilly day.

At the bottom of the scene is an odd, solid blue rectangle — perhaps this was to be a presentation piece that never got presented? Although a strong supporter of the arts and crafts of the region, Gagnon was not pleased when renditions of his paintings appeared without his permission, whether it be a painting or a hooked rug — he viewed it as a copyright infringement, a concept the local villagers did not understand. Speculation is that the blue rectangle was intended to contain information about the painting and the artist, however, Gagnon refused permission. The rug with its solid blue plaque then left Quebec for Rhode Island, where it stayed for many years.

Quebec hooked rug, 7' x 9', 1940-1950. After a painting "Laurentian Village" by Clarence Gagnon, 1927, currently in the collection of Musée des Beaux Arts, Quebec.

SILAS PATTERSON HEART TABLE

In the master bedroom is a two-drawer lamp table found near Wolfville, Nova Scotia, in original surface with a folky heavy-cut maple inlay on the drawer fronts and an inlaid maple heart centred on the top. An old tag found with the table is inscribed as follows: "Made by Silas Patteson [sic] 1830 Canning". On the reverse of the tag: "Built Victoria Inn Wolfville for William Chase". William Chase was a pioneer in the apple business in Annapolis Valley and one of the wealthiest men in Nova Scotia at the time. His house, known as the Chase House built in 1893, exemplifies the Victorian vernacular style and today is a historic property known as the Victoria Inn in Wolfville.

According to ancestry research, a Silas Patterson was born in Hants County in 1827 and died in Canning in 1902. Follow-up research with historians in the area reveals that Silas Patterson is listed in *McAlpine's Nova Scotia Directory* of both 1869 and 1896 as a carpenter in Canning. He is also found in *Canada, Seafarers of the Atlantic Provinces, 1789-1935* as owner of a brigantine named *Niagra* (1866), where he is listed as a tradesman, non-marine.

In 1871 and 1881 the Canning census lists Silas as a carpenter; the 1891 census identifies his home as Sheffield Mills (near Canning) with the occupation of carpenter/moulder; by 1901 he is listed as a retired carpenter. The mention of him being a carpenter/moulder is significant because it shows an elevation of his status related to his woodworking capabilities. With William Chase being a man of high stature he certainly would have selected an accomplished and experienced contractor for his grand house.

All this background supports the theory that this is the same Silas Patteson mentioned on the tag and suggests that the table could date no earlier than the 1840s if Silas began his career as an apprentice woodworker at the normal age of 14-16.

The table is birch with the original pine top; the two drawers are graduated in size, the larger being on top, each featuring two large horizontal inlaid maple diamonds that are positioned to completely fill the space between the two original pulls. The leg turnings begin mid-point down the post and are well executed in a robust Sheraton style terminating in a turned pad foot, a feature found on other Nova Scotia tables of this period. The inlay is more naively executed than the rest of the table, suggesting that Patterson's skill at the time was more in creating rather than detailing, but fortunately this is what gives the table its folky charm with the sideways heart centred on the top and the bold double diamonds on each drawer.

Have we unearthed a previously unknown Nova Scotia cabinetmaker with more of his furniture resting anonymously in collections waiting to be discovered, or was this a "one-off" table that Silas Patterson made for himself?

Nova Scotia, 1845-1850.

DECORATED CANOE PADDLE

"Way out", it says on the grip of the paddle — just in case you get really lost! And that would have been easy to do given that the area being explored was a vast wilderness of forests and lakes in 1890.

This paddle with the detailed and beautifully executed map of the river system leading to the headwaters of the Ottawa River is more than a beautiful memento of a canoe trip — it in fact documents a scouting trip for timber made by J.B. Charleson at a time when he was a forest ranger for the province of Quebec (confirmed in the 1891 Board of Trade journal of Great Britain). Charleson was born in Quebec to Scottish parents in 1836 and was quickly baptised John Baptiste by the local parish priest since the infant wasn't expected to live and the parents hadn't chosen a name.

The frailty didn't last however; at the age of fifty-four Charleson's scouting trip took him some 530 kilometres northeast of Mattawa, Ontario, and covered some 3200 square kilometres of wilderness. By the time he reached his "way out" he had identified accessible tracts of timber with a value in 1890 of over $1,000,000.

Further research reveals that J.B. Charleson's adventures in exploring Canadian frontiers didn't end with this canoe trip — in 1899 he was commissioned to supervise the construction of the telegraph line in the Yukon, deemed a critical link for the Northwest Mounted Police at the time of the Klondike Gold Rush where a "wild west" lifestyle prevailed.

This is a piece of folk art that truly speaks — a canoe paddle that has taken us on a totally different route than intended — and through it we have learned about a man who played a role in two significant events in Canada's development at the turn of the 20th century.

HOOKED RUGS

Hand-hooked rag rugs originally destined for the cold winter floor are today often elevated to the status of wall art by seasoned collectors who value them for their freedom of expression in colour and design. The rugs often tell a story, perhaps of a family business, a favourite animal or a historic event; geometric rugs are stunning in their modernity, perfectly at home in a downtown condo. Driven by the nature of materials on hand, imagery can range from an academic theorem style of floral patterns to Oriental rug themes and a limitless variety of whimsical designs and colours.

Traditionally made using strips of rags from old clothes and blankets, hooked rugs became popular at all levels of society as rug patterns and when materials became readily available from commercial vendors and catalogues in the late 19th century. Given their intended use and the nature of the materials used, it is a testament to the technical and artistic skills of the makers that so many of these decorative rugs have survived.

Rug hooking had long been a domestic pursuit in eastern Canada, with reports of floors in Newfoundland being covered from wall to wall with layers of hooked mats to keep the cold wind at bay. Both women and men were involved, with the men often sketching out geometric designs, gathering materials, and sometimes doing the hooking as well.

By the early 20th century the tradition in Canada was international news as hooked rugs were gaining in popularity due to the commercial output of studios such as that of Georges-Édouard Tremblay in Charlevoix, Quebec, and the rugs marketed internationally by the Grenfell Mission in Newfoundland and Labrador.

Early hand-hooked rugs, whether they be from a pattern or unique, are highly sought after by collectors and may sell for significant sums, but there are many excellent examples on the market today compatible with all budgets and tastes. Whether it is on the wall or at the foot of a bed, a well preserved and mounted hooked rug is an easy and affordable way to give a room a special feel.

Nova Scotia Trapunto Rug

In the master bedroom is this charming hooked rug of a farmyard scene. Hooked in the trapunto style where longer material is clipped to create raised "puffy" sections, this rug is full of colour and life with its naive perspective.

The similarity of this rug to one featured in McKendry's *Folk Art: Primitive and Naive Art in Canada* is uncanny, with the same red-headed little girl, the same pink house, the same apple tree, and the same floral lined walkway and floral wreath framing technique — undoubtedly by the same hand. The most significant difference being that in one rug the little girl is looking out to sea and in the other she is surrounded by her farm yard friends.

Nova Scotia, circa 1900, wool and burlap.

Grenfell Industries

What started as a medical mission in the 1890s for Dr. Grenfell to assist people living in the isolated outport communities of Newfoundland and Labrador eventually became a successful community enterprise selling hooked mats to the elite of Canadian and American society. For decades Grenfell Industries provided an economic boost to the Newfoundland and Labrador region.

At first the designs were limited but soon artists were engaged to develop new images to reflect the magnificent land, birds, animals, and seascape of the area. During the fishing off-season the Grenfell Mission also engaged the local men to carve wood and ivory items to complement the mats. Aside from Canada and England, key markets were developed in Boston, Philadelphia, Vermont and New York — not an easy accomplishment given the geography and transportation difficulties at that time. Although the market softened by the mid-20th century, Grenfell Industries remains in St. Anthony, Newfoundland, where a limited supply of hooked mats and accessories are still produced each year.

Flying Mallards and Canoe

The decor in the master bedroom reflects the peace and tranquility of another time principally through the imaginative use of three hooked rugs as wall art: a large Clarence Gagnon scene of a Quebec village in winter, a trapunto style rug of a busy Nova Scotia farmyard, and a colourful Grenfell rug of an early morning vista with mallard ducks in flight.

Adding to the fantasy of the third is the way the objects have been assembled: the ascending ducks in the rug are joined by carved wooden counterparts in original paint from Quebec, circa 1930, mounted on the wall. The imagery gives the viewer the impression that the ducks were all startled by the approaching quill-decorated canoe that seems to be slicing silently through the bull rushes in the foreground of the rug. The birch bark model canoe is made in the voyageur style with excellent floral quill decoration and gunwales wrapped in spruce root. Circa 1890, the canoe model was found on Manitoulin Island, Ontario.

Maria Laplante Joyal (1901-1986)

Most people can't help but smile when they see a rug hooked by Maria Laplante Joyal. The obvious familiarity of the artist with her subject, the love of the land and home, the colourful scenes, and a subtle sense of humour are all elements found in her rugs. Naive expression from an untrained hand, each rug tells a story of life — its trial and tribulations — as interpreted by Mme Joyal.

Maria Laplante Joyal lived a quiet life as a farmer's wife in St-Louis-de-Richelieu in Quebec, hooking rugs in her spare time for her family and friends until being discovered by antique pickers in the 1960s. It was Nettie Sharpe, as quoted in *Les Paradis du Monde* by Pascale Galipeau, who encouraged Mme Joyal and told her she would buy every rug she made. Over ten years Mrs. Sharpe bought some 950 rugs. With this kind of output she would have had little time for anything else so it is highly possible that Mme Joyal engaged family members or close friends to hook rugs in her style and thereby share in the new-found fortune.

The rugs gained fame before anyone knew her name, identified by Nettie Sharpe as only a rug maker near Sorel, but today she is immediately recognized as the artist of these unique rugs with their catchy titles:

"*J'aime la vitesse*" (I like speed), says one fish to another, "*Pas moi*" (Not me), says the little one in response.

"*Le Boeuf de Blouin*" (Blouin's ox) identifies the scene as logs are hauled out of the woods on a sleigh, surrounded by stumps as big as a man.

"*Allo mon Pit*", says the girl to her beau guiding his horse and plough in a field with three apple trees in the distance and a single flower in the foreground. "*Bonjour Zezette*", he says in response with a smile on his face. Perhaps a tribute to a budding romance witnessed by Mme. Joyal.

Hooked rugs by Maria
Laplante Joyal.

Commemorative Rug — Phoebe Heise

Warming the floor in the guest room is a commemorative hooked rug created by Phoebe Heise to honour the coronation of Queen Elizabeth II in June 1953. With elaborate details including the royal carriage, crown jewels, orb and sceptre, swords, and other symbols of the British monarchy surrounding a large central medallion with the crown and initials ER, the rug is both formal and folky at the same time. The curious alignment of the sword tips and hilts as the blades slip under the circular medallion provides visual relief to what was intended to be a serious homage to the Queen.

Phoebe Heise (Mrs. H.C. Heise) lived in the Ottawa area and spent summers at Silver Islet, an old mining town near Thunder Bay. Treasured by the family, in 1977 the Phoebe Heise rug was selected to be one of 138 exhibits in *A Silver Jubilee Salute to Her Majesty the Queen* organised by the Imperial Order Daughters of the Empire (IODE) in honour of the royal visit to Ottawa. "The rug was our most interesting exhibit — the Queen took notice of it too," commented one organizer to Phoebe.

That was all Phoebe needed to hear.

MISS MADILLA SMITH — E. S., PAINTER

Signed Canadian portraits are rare; to find one with the sitter identified is rarer still. Hanging over a Quebec inlaid butternut chest of drawers is a portrait of *Miss Madilla Smith, aged 17,* as written in colourful script on the reverse side. The name alone makes her an interesting mystery, but it is more intriguing with the other inscription on the back: *E.S., Painter.*

Painted in a classic itinerant style, the portrait was discovered in the 1990s in the attic of an early homestead in Woodstock, Ontario, and shows a rather serious young girl with deep brown eyes who seems mature beyond her 17 years.

Fascinated with the brief background and the few clues, diligent sleuthing revealed Madilla Mary as the seventh of nine children of Charity Alberta Smith of Ancaster, Ontario, and William Smith (1786-1856) also of Ancaster. The parents' marriage in 1809 was said to unite two distant Smith clans. William Smith was the grandson of an American who came to Canada from New Jersey in 1787 as an early settler of Grimsby Township, while Madilla's maternal grandfather, John Smith, moved his family (ten children including Madilla's mother) to Ancaster in 1798.

Further digging identified E.S. as Ezekiel Sexton (1820-1859) who moved to the same town of Ancaster from New York State in 1830. Ezekiel apparently earned his living as an itinerant painter throughout the southwestern Ontario region and also farmed near London, Ontario. According to Museums London, he may have received some art training from a family member, Samuel Hayden Sexton, a painter in Schenectady, New York, who worked in a similar style. Unfortunately the nature of the artist lured Ezekiel to the California Gold Rush and he is believed to have died there searching for his fortune in 1859.

Another painting by Ezekiel Sexton is a self-portrait with his wife and daughter (circa 1852) in the collection of Museums London. Although listed as an artist/painter, no other works by Sexton are known to the author.

Oil on canvas painting by Ezekiel Sexton, Ontario, circa 1840.

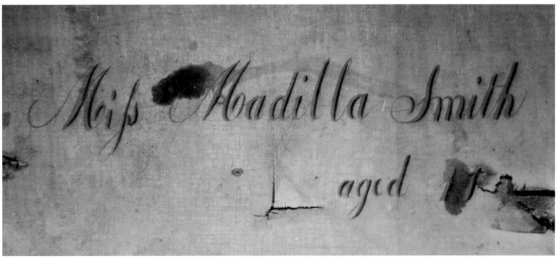

QUEBEC CHEST OF DRAWERS

Greeting guests in the spare bedroom with Madilla Smith (see previous discussion) is a Quebec butternut chest of drawers in the Hepplewhite style with inlaid drawer fronts and flared French feet.

This is a very stylish piece of furniture of good scale and proportions. Refinished to the natural butternut patina with the exception of the black painted quarter columns and original ebonized pulls, the chest also features a shaped skirt and graduated drawers. Of importance is the maple inlay on the drawers, an unusual and dramatic feature on a mid-19th century piece of Quebec country furniture.

There are several Quebec chests of drawers known of similar form and inlaid decoration: several are dated, many have floral motifs in the centre of the drawers, all are butternut and all are in the Hepplewhite style. It was long believed that these chests came from the region east of Levis on the south side of the St. Lawrence past Bellechasse. But in 1995 the *Upper Canadian* published an article by Merlin Acomb, a friend and ardent researcher, presenting a convincing theory that these chests were likely the output of a Magloire Garon who operated a furniture shop in Saint-Michel-de-Bellechasse in 1851 and was previously listed as a furniture maker in Quebec City from 1834-1847. Importantly, as the article states, Garon was also described as an *ébiniste*, a distinction that identifies a skilled craftsman who can work with veneers and different woods.

The chest of drawers in the collection features a maple linen-fold line inlay on all drawer fronts and an inlaid swirling "good luck" charm centred on the lower drawers. The quality of the inlay, combined with the style and size of the chest, suggests the same maker as those chests previously mentioned and attributed to Magloire Garon.

Quebec, 1830-1850.

THOMAS NISBET LEGISLATIVE DESK

When it was announced that this desk would be for sale at a New Brunswick auction a few years ago it created quite a stir — the knowledgeable collector community knew that it was without a doubt a rare piece of furniture produced in the shop of one of Canada's most accomplished furniture makers of the early 19th century, Thomas Nisbet of Saint John.

Thomas Nisbet arrived in New Brunswick from Scotland in 1812 as a trained cabinet maker. Settling in the growing city of Saint John, he quickly capitalized on the burgeoning need for high quality furniture and by 1816 he was competing with American imports and serving customers from Fredericton as well. Nisbet made formal furniture, working with local birch, maple, and pine in addition to importing "show" woods, primarily dark mahogany from the West Indies, for his best pieces.

Nisbet's reputation quickly grew as his shop produced both standard and custom-made furniture including banquet tables, chairs, sewing stands, sofa tables, and chests of drawers. Nisbet is known to have labelled some of his furniture; however, with time, paper labels deteriorate and 200 years later very few labelled pieces are known. Attributions become even more muddy since many Nisbet pieces made their way into the U.S. in the mid-20th century and were sometimes "re-branded" as Boston or New York cabinetry due to the high quality of Nisbet's work.

Buying local was a popular theme in the early 19th century and Nisbet certainly benefited when Sir Howard Douglas, lieutenant-governor of New Brunswick from 1823-1831, offered him a contract to build furniture for Government House. Although unlabelled, the legislative desk in the collection is identical to a labelled example and other known examples. Thomas Nisbet likely designed the desks while teams of apprentices completed the large order. Constructed in mahogany in the Regency style, they were made to be functional and sturdy, perhaps explaining the relatively heavy base with the transverse support strengthened by the turned vertical balusters.

Legislative desk by Thomas Nisbet, Saint John, New Brunswick, 1825-1830.

JOSEFINA

Rescued from a garbage dump in Annapolis County, Nova Scotia, Josefina looks like a woman who was a lot of fun. With her tilted head, rosebud mouth, and billowing blouse she appears to be ready to raise her skirt off the floor to dance a jig rather than posing for a personal portrait.

Josefina is painted in the "reverse painting on glass" style where the artist must commence with the objects in the foreground and then add the layers behind in order, painting the background as the last element. Very complex theorem paintings were common subjects for this genre, often combined with tinsel to achieve a three-dimensional effect.

Identified simply as *Josefina*, the work is naively executed in the folk portrait style of the 1840 period.

Exhibited as #116 in the *Spirit of Nova Scotia* exhibition in 1982.

Josefina

HALIFAX DRESSING TABLE

Situated in an upstairs guest bedroom is an unusual side table with two shallow drawers separated by a hinged door that accesses a large storage compartment, all with brass hardware. The upper drawer is false, likely included for visual balance, while the lower drawer is functional. Of special interest is a pop-up mirror at the rear of the top, still retaining the original glass and the original wooden latching mechanism. The mirror performed the dual purpose of either reflecting the viewer's image or reflecting the light of a candle to brighten up the room.

Several features support a theory that this could be from the shop of John Tulles: the wood is a lighter mahogany typical of Tulles, although he certainly wasn't the only Halifax cabinetmaker who preferred it

over the darker mahogany used by Thomas Nisbet of New Brunswick. Other Tulles influences can be seen in the finely turned Sheraton legs and the rectilinear light coloured line inlay on the posts. But the final bit of evidence is the complexity of the piece itself; with the pop-up mirror, inlay, and construction details, this would have been a difficult piece of furniture to make in the 1815-25 period. Considering the other tell-tale signs along with the sophisticated design, it seems reasonable to suggest that this dressing cabinet would be the output of the finest cabinetmaker of the area — John Tulles.

For more details on John Tulles, see the discussions of the card table (page 76) and side chair (page 80) featured earlier in this book.

HORSE AND BUGGY — PUNKEYDOODLES CORNERS

Although antique folk art carvings can be expensive, there are many excellent examples by contemporary carvers readily available on the marketplace. The trick is to differentiate the good from the not so good, and the best way to do that is to study the classic examples first and talk to dealers and collectors — then apply the criteria of form, colour, detail, charm, and budget to make a selection.

This wonderful carving by Jacob Roth, a Mennonite carver from western Ontario but born in Punkeydoodles Corners in Waterloo County, shows a red horse pulling a four-wheeled buggy with the driver and passenger wearing their "Sunday best". Mr. Roth had a busy life farming, raising a family and making ends meet the best way he could. It wasn't until he slowed down in the late 1970s at the age of 82 that he took up the pastime of creating sculpture. With no formal training he did what he loved, not for money or fame but just for his own pleasure — a true folk artist. His carriages and other conveyances are especially well executed reflecting his earlier employment installing rubber on wagon wheels and a life-long interest in machinery.

Jacob Roth stopped carving in his early 90s and in 1992 several of his works were purchased by the Canadian Museum of History. The carving in this collection was purchased at an antique show from a high-profile dealer in 2000 for a very affordable $250.

Carving by Jacob Roth (1896-1995), Tavistock, Ontario.

LONGPRÉ BIRD SHELF

A few decades ago a Quebec picker purchased, for a very reasonable sum, a stack of mouldings from a house on Gouin Boulevard in Montreal, only to discover that they all had prominent colourful carvings of birds under the layers of overpaint. Some of the mouldings next appeared at a dealer picker auction "in the rough", selling again for a relatively reasonable sum, but as soon as the first one appeared restored to its original surface their importance and desirability soared.

Created by a carver only known as A. Longpré, the architectural pieces look like wall shelves with birds exquisitely carved and painted as decoration. Most of the known "shelves" have two birds (often with a different bird on each end), while the one in this collection features a carved downy woodpecker in the centre of a shaped backboard. The bird is flanked by acanthus leaf scrolls and stippled back surface in blue paint.

The shelf had been painted over, but the bird was thankfully left untouched in its original surface.

Quebec, circa 1900.

TIMBER SHANTY

Looking through the windows one almost feels like "a peeping Tom" as the faces of the long-ago lumberjacks stare right back at you, as if you had distracted them from their dinner or conversation.

The shanty's dark outside logs seem cold in contrast to the interior, where loaves of fresh baked bread are seen and supplies line the walls of the building while two large cast iron stoves occupy the centre. Many of the supplies are labelled just like the originals dating from the 1890-1910 period: tea, coffee, and baking powder from the Blue Ribbon Manufacturing Company (Winnipeg, Manitoba); sugar from Dominion Granulated Sugar (Wallaceburg, Ontario); starch from the Canada Starch Company (Cardinal [Edwardsburg], Ontario), flour from Robin Hood (formerly the Moose Jaw Milling Company), and there is even some Vicks VapoRub on hand for colds and aching muscles.

The shanty was a place of rest for the hardy lumberjacks, surrounded by trees sometimes reaching the height of a 20-storey building and measuring up to 16 feet in circumference. Felled by axe until the 1870s when the lumberjack's life improved with the introduction of the two-man buck saw, it is no wonder that the shanty became a place for storytelling and demonstrations of feats of strength or endurance to help pass the time. It was a melting pot of cultures and testosterone with legends like the Ottawa Valley lumberjack Jos Montferrand, who was immortalized for his bravado in the song "Big Joe Mufferaw" by Canadian country singer Stompin' Tom Connors.

Canada's vast tracts of timber have always played a key role in the economic prosperity of the land: the abundant forest was key to the longevity of the early settlers because timbers were used domestically for fortification and were also shipped to France or England as ballast to be used in ship building, construction, and even furniture making. In the 1850-1900 period the Canadian lumber industry boomed with domestic and foreign demand, which gradually turned these remote logging camps into communities with roads, housing, and secondary businesses. At the time of Confederation the lumber industry employed tens of thousands of workers throughout eastern Canada. Today the forestry sector annually contributes some $20 billion to the Canadian economy.

This model illustrates a timber shanty in the early 1900s, a home to the lumberjacks for months at a time — complete with kitchen, dining room, and sleeping quarters all under one roof. Exceptional in its detailed interior, this model was likely made by someone who lived and worked in a lumber camp.

Found near Timmins, Ontario, 1930-1940.

LOGGING SCENE — JULIUS HÜMME

On the wall to the left of the timber shanty is an Ontario winter logging scene painted by Julius Hümme, a German immigrant to Canada in 1864 who settled in the District of Muskoka, Canada West, near Sparrow Lake. In 1868 Hümme opened a photography studio in Orillia where he remained until the early 1880s when he then moved to Toronto and opened an art studio for his painting. He is known to have worked in both watercolour and oil. This painting of the logging scene with timber shanty is oil on canvas signed in the bottom right with his monogram JH.

Another painting by Hümme — *Indian Encampment with Dogs* — is illustrated in *Folk Art: Primitive and Naive Art in Canada*, page 92, by Blake McKendry. Information on Julius Hümme was sourced from the *East Georgian Bay Historical Journal*, 1981, page 68.

CARVED DEER

Found in the grandkids' bedroom with the timber shanty model and three iron beds is a carved doe with turquoise bead eyes and lifelike original paint. By positioning the deer on the desk with a painting directly behind depicting a resting buck and doe gives the illusion that our deer has just emerged from the scene — great stimulation for young minds!

This is a good example of Quebec folk carving in the late 19th century where the artist has captured the essence of the subject with minimal detail. The extension of the neck, the long legs, the slight twist to the head, the erect ears and of course the piercing eyes all give this deer an alert quality so typical of their behaviour in nature.

Originally part of the Wiser Distillery Canadiana collection that was started in 1965 — likely with the impetus of recognizing the Centennial of Confederation in 1967 — the deer was deaccessioned by the company with the rest of the collection in the late 1990s. This deer was acquired for this collection at the Toronto Downtown Antiques Show in 2001.

Quebec, circa 1880.

MAIN STREET WINNIPEG — E.J. HUTCHINS

A watercolour on paper depicting Main Street, Winnipeg, around 1870, painted by Ernest J. Hutchins, shows two Native tents on the outside of town with the new settlement slowly taking shape in the distance.

Hutchins enjoyed bringing back the past in his paintings, most of which he painted in the 1910 period. Active in Winnipeg, his paintings reflect mountain scenes and the vanishing Prairie landscape with forgotten forts, buildings long ago abandoned, and geographic vistas that have disappeared forever. His work is included in the collection of the Royal Ontario Museum.

Inscribed *Main Street Winnipeg* 1870, painted circa 1910.

THE STEAMSHIP S.S. *QUEBEC*

A naive painting of the steamship S.S. *Quebec* with black smoke billowing out of its stack while navigating the ice floes of the St. Lawrence River just below the Citadel of Quebec City. Although the artist has successfully captured the mood of cold and danger, the folk art charm of the painting is still evident in both scale and perspective as illustrated by the leaning Citadel fortifications that appear poised to slide down the icy cliff.

Quebec, watercolour, unsigned, late 19th century.

INDIAN MOTHER AND HUNTER — D. GALE

Several 19th century artists copied the style of well-known Quebec artist Cornelius Krieghoff as exhibited in this pair of oval watercolours by Denis Gale (1828-1903) showing a winter scene of a mother with child facing left in one painting and, in the other, the hunter with his rifle heading in the opposite direction. Both are attired in traditional colourful Native dress, the man sporting a sash and red garters.

Gale arrived in Quebec City in 1833. He was initially involved in the lumber business and became a friend of Krieghoff, who at that time was at the height of his popularity as an artist. Gale is known to have sketched and produced watercolours of habitants and Indian life in the Krieghoff style during the 1855-65 period and then moved to Colorado in the 1880s.

CHAPTER 6

Mud Room/Stairwell

A rig of oversize yellowlegs shorebirds stand on a blue Quebec buffet alongside a three-dimensional bakery trade sign in the form of Little Jack Horner. This is the welcoming party as you enter the side door into the mud room, a place to kick off boots and hang coats on hooks.

A back stairway to the second floor provides a perfect display wall for the collection of colourful and graphic game boards. Complementing the look on the opposite wall is a yellow Ontario buffet used for winter storage of hats and mitts, with an early carved bowl in blue paint on top and a folky tin bird tree on the wall behind.

NORFOLK COUNTY BUFFET

The dramatic high cut-out base and strong yellow paint give this buffet a unique impressive stature.

Finding the right yellow on a piece of furniture is not easy. Often the colour is at one extreme or the other: either too yellow or, more often than not, too close in colour to the wood underneath to stand out as original paint. On this buffet the yellow is stunning and the intensity of the piece is magnified by its crisp lines, subtle cock beading around the doors and drawers, original black knobs, and a dramatic Hepplewhite style high base.

Original throughout, with excellent patina to the pine where exposed by wear, the overpaint on this piece was removed by a dry scraping method to expose the strong yellow underneath.

Ontario, Norfolk County, circa 1835.

CANADIAN SHOREBIRDS

Like a lot of folk art, decoys were first created for utilitarian purposes — in this case by market hunters as a tool of the trade. These decoy makers were proud of their creations as far as they "look like a duck" but they never saw themselves as artists until later years when collectors recognized the sculptural merits inherent in these working birds. Today decoy carvings, including shorebirds, are passionately pursued by collectors searching for the elusive maker or species, as well as by enthusiasts looking for the perfect small sculpture to fill a window sill or to place on a small table.

Shorebird decoys are extremely sculptural as they originally had either heavy wire legs or a long stick dowelled into the belly that naturally elevates the form. Unlike duck decoys generally designed to float on the water, shorebird decoys such as yellowlegs, snipes, curlews, and plovers were planted on the shore with the long legs pushed into the sand as part of a "rig" (group of decoys) placed to attract the flock.

Yellowlegs Root Head shorebird by William Rowlings (1891-1962) Musquodoboit Harbour, Nova Scotia, circa 1920.

Naive decoys such as this one have a certain charm in their simplistic execution and are proof that the artistry found in many decoys was done purely for the love rather than for a need to make the most realistic lures possible. For example, early Native decoys were often fashioned from bunches of reed or sticks, just enough to get a duck's attention.

The head of this decoy was created from a pine branch and then mounted on a simple carved body that was quickly painted in black with a white belly and yellow eyes. According to Dale and Gary Guyette in *Decoys of Maritime Canada*, William Rowlings only carved about 50-60 root head yellowlegs and plovers.

PEI Golden Plover from the eastern shore of Malpeque Bay, Prince Edward Island. This is a well-executed bird carved in full body with a split tail, wide head, original paint and tack eyes. The heavy splotching of black paint up the creamy white breast and neck draws attention to the head creating a mask-like band of white around the tack eyes.

Stylistically this carved plover bears certain characteristics, including the wide flat-top head, tack eyes and split tail, that are also found in shorebirds carved along New England's Massachusetts shore.

This shorebird is illustrated on page 140 of *Decoys of Maritime Canada* by Dale and Gary Guyette.

Red Knot Decoy, Toronto, circa 1880, from the rig of Thomas Southam.

Now filled in as part of the industrial Toronto waterfront, Ashbridge's Bay in Toronto Harbour was an ideal area for shorebirds to gather in the 19th century. The Ashbridge's Bay area was also the home of Thomas Southam, who made his living working on the lake as an avid hunter and sportsman. It is not known if Southam carved his own decoys, but this Red Knot is one of a few documented as being from the rig of birds used by him in Toronto Harbour in the late 19th century.

The Red Knot is a medium size shore bird but the second largest of the sandpiper group. Winter plumage is a light grey but in breeding season the plumage is mottled grey on top with a cinnamon coloured throat and breast, With expected wear as a working bird, this full-bodied shorebird retains its original bill and wire legs as well as original "breeding season" paint with feather detailing and a rusty-red breast.

Ex collection Mrs. Marjorie McConnell, Montreal.

Toronto Plover Decoy, beautifully carved in full body form with a quality old second surface paint. Mounted on a contemporary base, this sculptural bird retains its glass eyes and original bill.

Circa 1880.

Peep Decoy from the former rig of Thomas Southam, noted sportsman from Toronto.

Peep is the generic term for a small sandpiper; this superb decoy is carved in full body form with an extended neck, excellent stippled original paint and an elegant arched iron bill, mounted on a single iron rod for the legs.

Ex collection: Mrs. Marjorie McConnell, Montreal

John Ramsay (1858-1934), Summerside, PEI, circa 1910. A sleekly carved and highly sculptural hollow-bodied decoy with a slightly upturned "split" tail. In original paint with some effective cream-white stick-spatter markings on the black back, this decoy exhibits beautiful flowing form and is in very good as-found condition. Obviously "hunted over" the decoy has random shot marks, with some shot penetrating the hollow body, which provides an interesting rattling sound when shaken. The bill is an old replacement.

Rig of four Oversize Yellowlegs in original paint.

These shorebirds are characterized by their large scale and long extended necks, carved in the semi-round with split tails and long wooden bills. The paint is simply executed in cream-yellow and black, but with highly effective results. The varied stances are due to the position of the original placement holes on the bodies.

Originally found in Souris, Prince Edward Island, these decoys were probably used towards the centre of the Island in Malpeque Bay, circa 1900, an area where shorebirds gathered in the thousands. An apparent rig mate from Malpeque Bay is illustrated in *Decoys of Maritime Canada,* by Dale and Gary Guyette, page 136.

BAKERY TRADE SIGN — J. BOURGAULT

Little Jack Horner sat in the corner
Eating his Christmas pie.
He stuck in his thumb
And pulled out a plum,
And said, "What a good boy am I".

Sitting in the mud room entrance is Little Jack Horner eating his pie....

A favourite with the grandchildren, this almost life-size sculpture in a soft weathered white surface was the trade sign at a Montreal bakery shop for many years.

Carved by a member of a legendary family of Quebec carvers — Jacques Bourgault, son of Médard Bourgault (1897-1967) and nephew of André (1898-1958) and Jean-Julien (1910-1996). The Bourgault family was a pivotal force in establishing Quebec and the Saint-Jean-Port-Joli region in particular, as arguably the folk art capital of the continent in the early 20th century.

The sculpture is carved in one piece of laminated pine and is in very good condition, exhibiting minor age cracks and a missing spoon that is immediately replaced with one from the kitchen when the grandkids arrive.

Little Jack Horner is an English nursery rhyme that is based on a story that goes back to the days of Henry VIII. The legend says that Mr. Horner, as steward to the Bishop of Glastonbury, was asked to deliver twelve local land deeds as a Christmas gift from the bishop to the king so the Catholic monastery could be saved under Henry's new Protestant state. Glastonbury was the largest and wealthiest abbey in the kingdom.

The deeds were hidden in a pie to thwart any thieves encountered on the journey, but only eleven deeds apparently arrived, leading to speculation that Jack Horner may have had his fingers in the pie and pulled out the "plum" — the deed to the lands and manor house of Mells in Somerset. Horner claimed that he was granted the missing deed for his loyalty to the king; the bishop's "gift" didn't save the monastery, which was destroyed in 1539, the same year the bishop was executed for treason.

The Mells manor remained the home of the Horner family into the 20th century.

Quebec, signed Jacques Bourgault (1940-2017).

GAME BOARDS

Beginning the line of game boards on the wall up the staircase is an exceptional Quebec Parcheesi™ board in salmon-pink and yellow, each corner decorated with opposing geometric circles in yellow and dark green representing a compass star and Maltese cross.

At the centre of the board where "Home" is located in the game of Parcheesi is a square with a heavy black border that immediately focuses your attention on the scene of a landscape including a small French Canadian house with a tree and setting sun. The background sky is painted in the same yellow and salmon colour tones found on the board, and the green of the grass is the same green found in the geometric corners, creating a very harmonious composition.

Untouched dry surface, Quebec, circa 1870.
Ex collection Adrien Flibotte, Saint Hyacinthe, Quebec.

Quebec double-sided game board, 19th century.

Double-sided game board, 19th century.

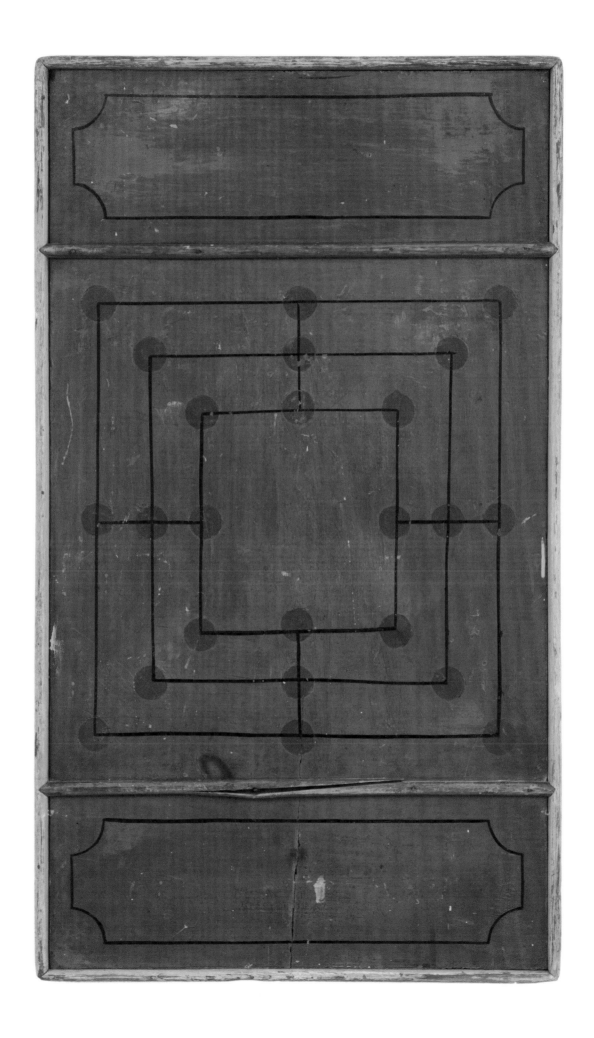

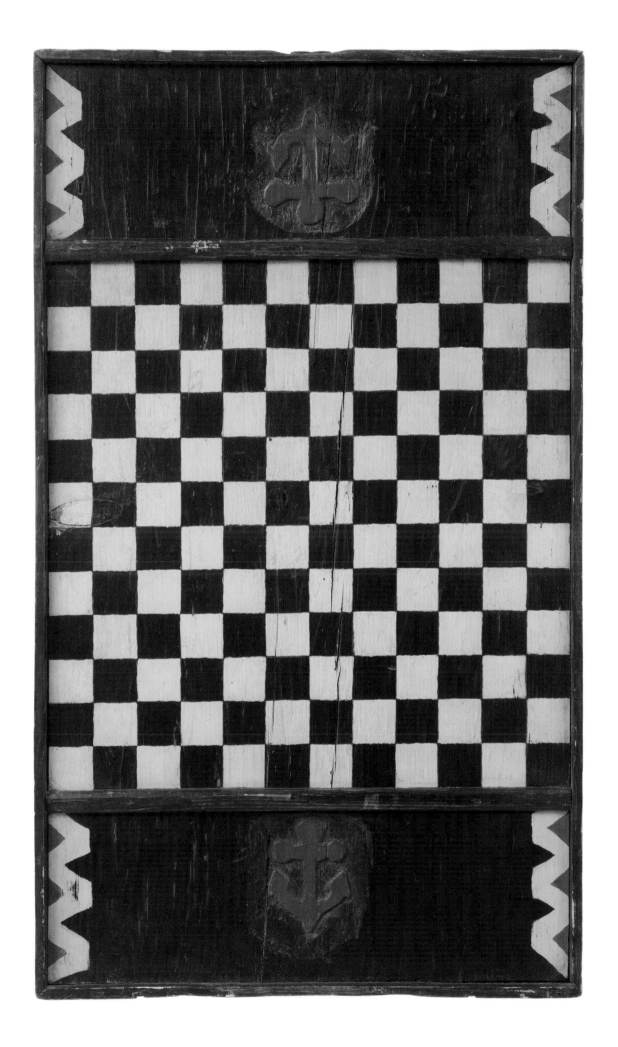

Double-sided game board, 19th century.

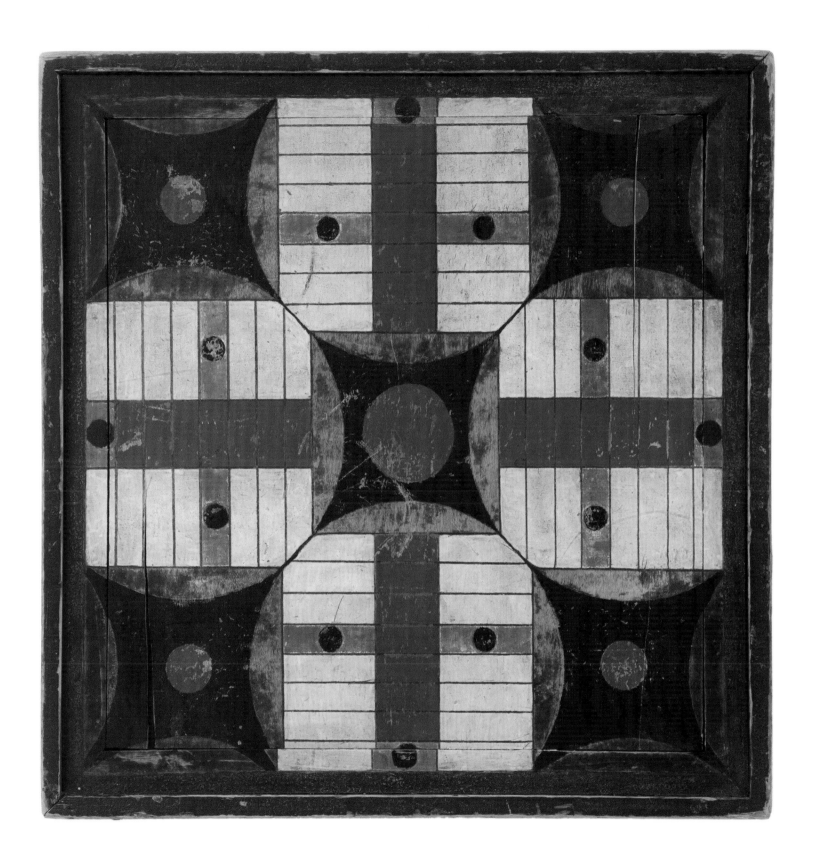

✦

CHAPTER 7

Family Room/Den

Primarily the grandkids' recreation room with an adult den to the side, this area has a strong nautical theme.

Two walls display several vibrantly coloured and boldly hooked rugs by noted Nova Scotia folk artist Deanne Fitzpatrick. Another wall features objects belonging to a New Brunswick ship captain who went on to launch an iconic Canadian company.

CAPTAIN ROBERT CHESTNUT

A portrait immediately gives a room a sense of history and a little mystery at the same time. It may even be amusing or contribute to a specific theme. Many of these 18th and 19th century portraits are anonymous, the names of their creator and the sitters long forgotten.

Fortunately we know a lot about this portrait of Captain Robert Chestnut of Fredericton, New Brunswick.

Centring a group of maritime-related objects in the basement recreation room, this portrait portrays Robert Chestnut as a man content with his life and his place in it. He is seated at his desk plotting a route on his Bay of Fundy chart, with a view of the Bay of Fundy directly out his window. In his left hand Captain Chestnut holds a parallel rule; the same parallel rule now rests on the 19th century blue stretcher base table below. The nautical theme also includes Captain Chestnut's telescope, acquired independently of the painting, importantly kept together to retain the legacy of Captain "Bob" as he is fondly known by the current custodians. Unfortunately, the whereabouts of the calipers that Captain Chestnut holds in his right hand is unknown.

Although Robert Chestnut was honoured for a daring sea rescue in 1828 and had crossed the Atlantic many times, he was more than an accomplished seaman; settling in New Brunswick in the 1830s, Chestnut began a successful merchant career, soon founding the Chestnut Hardware and Chestnut Canoe Company in Fredericton. The iconic Canadian company remained in the family until the 1960s when it was sold to the equally iconic Peterborough Canoe Company based in Ontario.

Artist unknown, oil on original canvas, New Brunswick, second quarter of the 19th century. Accompanying the portrait at auction were the following:

- The Chestnut family bibles dating back to 1797
- A marriage certificate of Robert Chestnut and Margaret Anthony
- Certificate of ownership of this portrait to the Chestnut family when it was on loan to the Chestnut Hardware Company in Fredericton

HOOKED RUGS — DEANNE FITZPATRICK

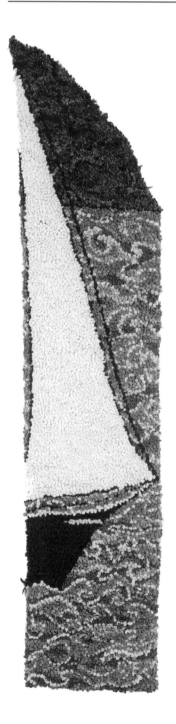

Hooked rugs by living Maritime artist Deanne Fitzpatrick dominate the basement playroom for the grandchildren, inspiring imagination and dreams. Her designs are bold and free-spirited, with a heavy textured surface that gives the image a three-dimensional feel.

The large rug at the centre of the grouping was a special order by the Burneys' four sons and depicts elements of the family's past and present, including a taxi representing Derek's youth in Fort William where he drove a taxi for his mother's taxi business and a church to the left representing Trinity Church in Port Arthur where Joan's father was minister.

Nautical scenes and an expressive colour palette pervade Fitzpatrick's works, reflecting her roots growing up in Placentia Bay, Newfoundland; she now lives and works near Amherst, Nova Scotia. As an authentic folk artist she creates her own designs and uses recycled cloth and old wool clothing from "real people in real communities".

MANITOBA PHEASANT

Early folk art from the western provinces is rare, as settlement of the region only started to flourish at the beginning of the 20th century.

This strutting pheasant carved by Robin Nipawin of Neepawa, Manitoba, is boldly painted, which time has aged to a beautiful crackled texture and mellow patina. The wooden legs are pegged into the base with the black feet painted on the flat green surface.

The pheasant was found in the Neepawa area, which is known for hunting; interestingly, in the Cree language, Neepawa translates as "Land of Plenty".

Manitoba Mennonite, circa 1910.

HORSE PULL TOY

Antique pull toys for children are either small in scale to be pulled along the floor or big enough for a toddler to hitch a ride. These carved black horses with white socks are of the latter variety, one complete with iron stirrups while the other still has the original bridle.

Both are handmade; the horse on the right is more folky with the small head, classic arched neck, and oversize body, the painted eyes and nostrils giving him a somewhat "mad" look. The carving still retains the original horsehair tail and is mounted on the original grey painted base with four cast iron wheels neatly hidden in slits cut into the platform.

Circa 1900.

BEAVER WEATHERVANE

From pre-settlement days until the end of the 19th century the beaver was an important economic and cultural symbol in Canada — idolized not only for the value of its pelts for garments and hats, but also for its work ethic and engineering skills. Much as the eagle is identified with the United States, today the beaver joins the maple leaf in worldwide recognition as an iconic Canadian symbol.

The beaver's popularity as an image reached its peak in the 19th century, appearing almost everywhere including English export dishware, on pewter spoons from Montreal, as furniture motifs and carvings, as design on hooked mats, on goblets as a symbol of the Saint-Jean-Baptiste Society in the 1880s, and as trade signs and weathervanes. Despite this popularity, the beaver had to wait until 1975 for official recognition as a national symbol.

The majority of beaver weathervanes are handmade, unlike other animal figures that were both handmade and commercially produced in copper and tin. In researching late 19th century American weathervane catalogues including Fiske, Washburn, Harris, Jones, Cushing, Buck, Westervelt, Mott, and Snow, numerous horses and roosters were available, as were farm animals of all descriptions, dogs, fish, deer, and peacocks, even a lion and an elephant, but no beaver was offered — perhaps too Canadian!

This handmade sheet metal beaver weathervane is of a good size in full form with a full bodied tail that is unusually placed in the naturalistic flat position rather than the more commonly found silhouette profile. Originally found proudly mounted on a Quebec barn in the 1960s, this vane retains its in-use barn paint and is original in all respects.

Quebec, 19th century.
Ex collection Charles Goodfellow, Léry, Quebec.

THE FENIAN RAIDS

The volunteer armed with his Enfield rifle stood anxiously at the water's edge with his fellow New Brunswick militiamen waiting for the Fenians to attack. Who were these Fenians? Why are they invading Canada after having just been through a divisive civil war in the United States? What is taking them so long to attack? Are they as tough as the rumours say?

Although minor in the sense of a foreign invasion of Canadian soil, the Fenian Raids that began at Campobello Island in New Brunswick in 1866 are considered by many historians as an important catalyst in securing Canadian Confederation in 1867.

The Fenian Brotherhood was a group of Irish nationalists in the United States disgruntled over Britain's rejection of Irish independence in 1865. With the end of the American civil war many Irish-born combatants joined the Fenian cause in launching attacks against British holdings in Canada East and Canada West. The idea was to use Canada as a bargaining chip in negotiations to achieve Ireland's independence from Britain.

The Enfield rifle in this collection is a Fenian Raid survivor, carried by a volunteer of the Canadian militia at the first Fenian raid at Campobello Island located in the Bay of Fundy just off shore from Lubec, Maine, where some 700 Fenians assembled in April 1866. It probably seemed like easy pickings for the battle-hardened Americans because Canada was still a loose network of regional jurisdictions that boasted a fledgling militia of volunteer, part-time soldiers in cavalry, infantry, and artillery units. The militia were eager but "green", although they were armed with the British-made Enfield rifle that at least provided equal firepower to the similar Springfield and Enfield rifles carried by the American invaders.

Repatriated by the Burney family from the United States in 2008, this Pattern 1853 Enfield is a long-barrel rifle, dated 1863 on the brass heel plate (three years before the Campobello raid) and is complete with leather sling, bayonet, and brass-mounted scabbard. Produced at the Royal Small Arms factory in Enfield, England, for line infantry use. British marks on the walnut stock indicate transfer from the Canadian militia to the Dominion of Canada in 1867 and a later mark shows retirement from military service. Most important, however, is the impressed mark on the scabbard: NB 2143. This simple mark indicates that this rifle was issued to the New Brunswick militia in 1863 and research shows that it was carried at Campobello Island as the local militia prepared to fend off the Fenians camped across the Bay.

Campobello was the first of five Fenian raids; however, it was short-lived as the show of militia strength on land and the appearance of British warships from Halifax was enough to convince the Fenians to disperse. This demonstration of "strength in numbers" provided by the British military is historically viewed as a decisive impetus for New Brunswick and other Atlantic provinces to join the forces of Confederation.

Featured above a New Brunswick birch slant front desk is a New Brunswick militia Enfield rifle used to defend against the Fenian invasion of Campobello Island in 1866.

The slant-front desk is a classic furniture form of the late 18th and early 19th centuries. Practical for its storage space and easily concealed workspace, the style dropped out of favour in the late 20th century as personal computers were too bulky to conveniently fit inside. Today the slant-front desk is slowly making a comeback as technology downsizes and the beauty and practicality of the form cannot be ignored.

Flanking the New Brunswick desk are two deck chairs manufactured near the end of the 19th century by the J.J. and D. Howe company of Saint John, New Brunswick.

The Fenian Raids in New Brunswick, Quebec, Ontario, and Manitoba occurred between 1866 and 1871 with only one victory for the Fenians in June 1866 near Fort Erie at the village of Ridgeway, Ontario. A small all-Canadian militia force was unable to repel the invaders; the Fenians, however, retreated to the United States before Canadian and British reinforcements arrived. Every other Fenian raid ended in failure, and the movement gradually collapsed.

The Enfield rifle was produced by the British from 1823 to 1880, as the standard issue weapon for various colonial militias and was also used by both the North and South in the U.S. Civil War. In late 1866 the British military introduced the Snider breech loading conversion that vastly improved reload time. The rifle in the collection was converted by the British military to a Snider Enfield Mark II some time after the Fenian raid at Campobello Island.

Fenian Raid Campaign Medal

Accompanying the Campobello Island Enfield rifle is a Canada General Service Medal initiated in 1899 and awarded to soldiers (both British regulars and local militia) and civilians who played a role during the Fenian Raids. Two medals were issued with the appropriate silver bar on a red/white/red ribbon indicating Fenian Raid 1866 or 1870. The image of Queen Victoria is on the obverse, and the reverse shows the national flag (the Red Ensign) and the word CANADA even though it is honouring an event that happened a year before Confederation was achieved.

With no relation to the rifle, this particular 1866 medal was awarded to Sergeant Major O. Jones, 14th Regiment, Princess of Wales' Own Regiment (PWOR). The unit was formed in 1863 from members of independent militia groups near Kingston, Ontario, as the 14th Battalion Volunteer Militia Rifles of Canada. The unit was re-named for the Princess following her wedding to the Prince of Wales (later Edward VII) the same year. The 14th Regiment fought in the Fenian Raid at Niagara in June 1866.

RECRUITMENT POSTERS

Found in the adult wing of the family room along with memorabilia from the Fenian Raids are three recruitment posters from the First World War. Collected today for their bold colours and strong design, antique and vintage posters produced since the late 19th century can be found at all budget levels and for virtually every field, from images of favourite locales to sports, entertainment, and propaganda.

In 1914, at the outbreak of the war, Canada had a military force of around 3,000 men. Soldiers were needed to support the allied force, but since Prime Minister Borden wanted to avoid invoking conscription for political reasons, recruitment posters for volunteers were created that could be prominently displayed in public facilities, factories, and shops. The initial posters concentrated on the excitement and brotherhood of volunteering, but as the fighting progressed the messaging became more pointed, with some even aimed at women (who still couldn't vote in federal elections) to convince their husbands and sons to join the cause.

Until 1916, when the Canadian government established the War Poster Service to produce posters in both English and French, recruitment posters were generally financed locally for district battalions and local regiments. Posters were also designed to appeal to various ethnic and religious groups or trades. The "Bushmen and Sawmill Hands" poster in the collection is a good example, designed to attract labourers with skills that were in short supply and urgently needed in Britain and France. Some 1,600 men, mainly from eastern Ontario, were recruited in just six weeks and went to Europe to clear terrain for airfields, prepare railway ties, and produce lumber for the building of trenches, barracks, and hospitals.

The recruitment campaign helped boost the ranks from 3,000 to over 300,000 volunteers just one year later. In total, some 650,000 Canadians and Newfoundlanders served in "The Great War"; over 62,000 were killed and an estimated 172,000 wounded.

Lest we forget.

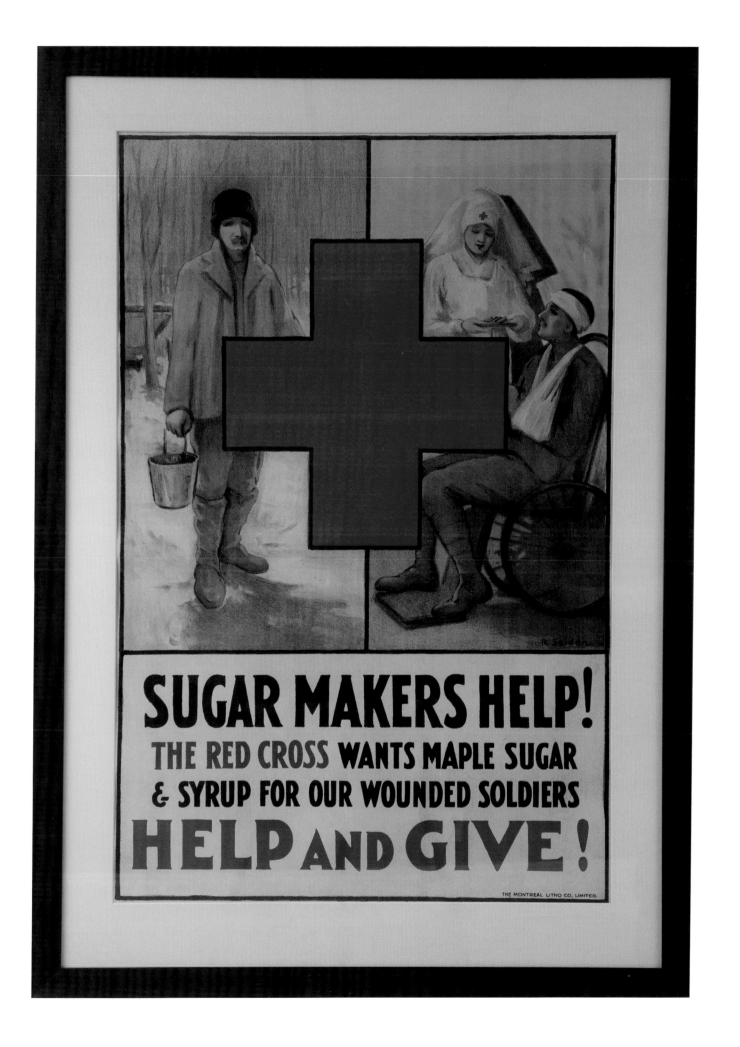

Acknowledgements

This book would not have been possible without the generosity and trust of Joan and Derek Burney in first agreeing with the concept and then giving me *carte blanche* to tramp through their home numerous times with photographer Marc Bider to record thoughts and images of the selected objects. Aside from the production hurdles over a three-year period in "getting it done", it was a distinct pleasure and the project provided a wonderful opportunity to expand my small area of expertise.

It is an honour to be associated with the Canadian Museum of History and Dundurn Press in this venture.

I thank Mark O'Neill, president and CEO of the museum, and Chantal Schryer, vice-president, corporate affairs, for their early support, as well as Bill Carman, the museum's manager, publishing and corporate products. Dundurn's Kirk Howard and Beth Bruder were enthusiastic from the outset, and I sincerely thank them and the rest of the Dundurn team for their professionalism and passion throughout the publishing process.

The financial support of several Canadian corporations was instrumental in moving this book forward and I thank them for joining in our celebration of Canada's 150th anniversary and 375 years of settlement in Montreal:

- GardaWorld
- Power Corporation of Canada
- PWL Capital
- Telus
- TransCanada PipeLines

Traditionally, an acknowledgements section is directly related to the preparation of the manuscript, design and publishing; however, I cannot with clear conscience, ignore those from my past whose expertise and passion brought me to the point where I could consider such an undertaking.

Numerous people have influenced my antiques career, but I give special tribute to only two: my early mentor Harriet Hawkins, antique dealer and passionate connoisseur of early painted furniture, and Nettie Sharpe, picker, dealer, collector, and noted authority on Quebec folk art.

Harriet Cuttle Hawkins took me under her wing as a young antiques picker/dealer. Through road trips as Harriet's driver in a constant search for "the best" I gained a deeper understanding of French Quebec culture and artefacts, cultivating my "eye" in the process. Nettie Sharpe is a well known name to collectors — her collection, knowledge and contributions to the antiques industry have helped promote Canadiana as a field worthy of international attention. For me, Nettie was equally influential with the stories of her early career as the first female picker who had the insight to locate, preserve, and identify some of Canada's most iconic pieces of early furniture and folk art. Mrs. Sharpe's passion began well before Canadiana gained the respect it deserved as a result of Jean Palardy's ground-breaking publication of *The Early Furniture of French Canada* in 1963, and subsequent public awareness related to Canada's centennial celebrations in 1967.

These two pioneering women led the charge in cultivating the notion in Canada of preserving original surface, colour, and provenance of early antiques and folk art. Mrs. Sharpe is referenced several times in *Celebrating Canada*, and the Nettie Covey Sharpe Personal Collection now resides at the Canadian Museum of History. A related museum website about Mrs. Sharpe and her collection is listed in the Bibliography.

I am equally indebted to my fellow professionals in the antiques community, arguably some of the most passionate people you will ever meet — unbeknownst to them, they have contributed greatly over the years to the expansion of my knowledge. With dramatic shifts in business demographics over the past decade, the antiques industry in Canada has consolidated, but the business remains buoyant due to these devoted professionals who bring remarkable inventory to market every day.

Several authors are mentioned in the introduction whose works have been a mainstay of my antiques education. I have referred to these books from my personal library in addition to other publications (identified in the bibliography), while online resources were used selectively to confirm and update information. All facts were double-checked as much as possible; however, I assume full responsibility for any errors of historical fact or dates.

I must also thank several individuals who assisted me with specific research: Wendy Donovan, deputy mayor of Wolfville, Nova Scotia, and Wendy Elliot, a Wolfville historian, for leading me to the town crier and historian, Gary Long, the source of much crucial information regarding Nova Scotia cabinet maker Silas Patterson; Kevin Puddister and Sandra Kiemele of the Dundas Museum for identifying the historic landmarks in the painting by J.R. Seavey; and Alison and Jamie Stalker for guidance on the shorebirds and providing welcome moral support.

The staff at the McCord Museum in Montreal — Karine Rousseau, Heather McNabb, and Céline Widmer — assisted me with background on the "Parrot on a Speckled Roost" that first appeared in a McCord exhibition in 1976. The next step was the Canadian Museum of History in Gatineau, Quebec, where the parrot was found, studied, and photographed thanks to the efforts of museum staff Elise Rowsome, Erin Gursky, Laura Sanchini, and Mélissa Duncan.

The manuscript review in both languages by author, collector, and academic John Fleming was much appreciated, as was his contribution to the French title. I am also indebted to colleague, friend, and author Michael Rowan for his invaluable insights and suggestions. Also to be thanked are John-Frederick Trenholm, Sandi Mielitz, and Linda and Doug Skinner for their editorial comments from different perspectives.

The sensitive photography of Marc Bider speaks for itself, and I thank him profusely for his professional approach and calming influence as we worked together to capture the essence of the objects while dealing with the challenges of a non-studio environment. I commend his sense of humour and commitment from the gestation stage to final production, with all the growing pains and challenges encountered along the way. I thank Jacqueline Dionne for her dedication and keen eye in revising the French manuscript and for its sensitive translation in collaboration with Jocelyne Benoît. I am also deeply indebted to Nathalie Cartier and her team for their expertise and commitment in helping us meet our deadline for the French edition.

I cannot conclude without thanking my spouse, Susan, for her encouragement and especially for looking the other way as I set aside domestic duties and immersed myself in this endeavour. Her eye for clean, uncluttered decor greatly influenced my thinking in preparing the manuscript. Her patience and support helped make this project possible.

PB

Select Bibliography

REFERENCE BOOKS/ARTICLES

Acomb, Merlin. "A Mystery Solved? — The Origin of the Quebec Inlay Chest of Drawers". *The Upper Canadian*, July/August 1995, 64-65.

Apfelbaum, Ben, Eli Gottlieb, and Steven J. Michaan. "Beneath the Ice, the Art of the Spear Fishing Decoy". New York: E.P. Dutton, Museum of American Folk Art, 1990.

Art Gallery of Nova Scotia. *Gameboards: An Exhibition of Canadian Gameboards of the 19th & 20th Centuries*. Halifax: Art Gallery of Nova Scotia, 1981.

Barbeau, Marius. *Ceinture Fléchée.* Montreal: Éditions l'Étincelle, 1973.

———. *Louis Jobin, statuaire*. Montreal: Librairie Beauchemin, 1968.

———. *Québec, où survit l'ancienne France*. Québec: Librairie Garneau, 1937.

Barbeau, Marius, et al. *The Arts of French Canada, 1613-1870*. Montreal/Detroit: Art Association of Montreal/Detroit Institute of the Arts, 1946.

Bird, Michael. *Canadian Country Furniture 1675-1950*. Toronto: Stoddart, 1994.

———. *Canadian Folk Art: Old Ways in a New Land*. Toronto: Oxford University Press, 1983.

Bird, Michael, and Terry Kobayashi. *A Splendid Harvest: Germanic Folk and Decorative Arts in Canada*. Toronto: Van Nostrand Reinhold, 1981.

Bishop, Robert. *American Folk Sculpture*. New York: E.P. Dutton, 1974.

Blais, Jacques. *La poterie et la céramique au Québec*. Saint-Anne-de-Beaupré, QC: Société du patrimoine et d'histoire de la Côte-de-Beaupré, 2009.

———. *L'art populaire au berceau de la Nouvelle France*. Saint-Anne-de-Beaupré, QC: Société du patrimoine et d'histoire de la Côte-de-Beaupré et de l'Île d'Orléans, 2013.

Blanchette, Jean-François. *Du coq à l'âme: l'art populaire au Québec*. Gatineau/Ottawa: Musée Canadien de l'histoire and Les Presses de l'Université d'Ottawa, 2014.

Blanchette, Jean-François, et al. *From the Heart: Folk Art in Canada*. Toronto: McClelland & Stewart with National Museum of Man, 1983.

Brasser, Ted J., and Judy Thompson. *"Bo'jou Neejee!": Profiles of Canadian Indian Art*. Ottawa: National Museum of Man, 1976.

Cameron, Christina, and Jean Trudel. *Québec au temps de James Patterson Cockburn*. Agincourt, ON: Gage Publishing for Les Éditions Garneau, 1976.

Chambers, Tim, and Selby Shaver. *The Art of the Game: A Collection of Vintage Game Boards from the Collection of Selby Shaver.* Massachusetts: Selby Shaver and Tim Chambers, 2001.

Collard, Elizabeth. *Nineteenth-Century Pottery and Porcelain in Canada.* Montreal: McGill University Press, 1967.

———. *The Potters' View of Canada.* Montreal/Kingston: McGill-Queen's University Press, 1983.

Comstock, Helen, ed. *The Concise Encylopedia of American Antiques.* New York/Toronto: Hawthorn Books/McClelland & Stewart, 1979.

Crépeau, Pierre. *Playing with the Wind: The Whirligig Collection of the Canadian Museum of Civilization.* Hull, QC: Canadian Museum of Civilization, 1991.

Dobson, Henry and Barbara Dobson. *The Early Furniture of Ontario & the Atlantic Provinces.* Toronto: M.F. Feheley, 1974.

———. *Heritage Furnishings of Atlantic Canada; A Visual Survey with Pertinent Points.* Kingston: Quarry Press, 2010.

———. *A Provincial Elegance: Arts of the Early French and English Settlements in Canada.* Kitchener-Waterloo: Kitchener-Waterloo Art Gallery, 1982.

Dunbary, Nancy J., ed. *Images of Sport in Early Canada.* Montreal and Kingston: McGill-Queen's University Press, 1976.

Ewing, Douglas. *Pleasing the Spirits: A Catalogue of a Collection of American Indian Art.* New York: Ghylen Press, 1982.

Fales, Dean A., Jr. *American Painted Furniture 1660-1880.* New York: E.P. Dutton, 1972.

Field, Richard Henning. *Spirit of Nova Scotia: Traditional Decorative Folk Art 1780-1930.* Toronto: Dundurn Press, 1985.

Finlayson, R.W. *Portneuf Pottery and Other Early Wares.* Toronto: Longman Canada, 1972.

Fitzpatrick, Deanne. *Hook Me a Story: The History and Method of Rug Hooking in Atlantic Canada.* Halifax: Nimbus, 1999.

Fleming, John A. *The Painted Furniture of French Canada, 1700-1840.* Camden East, ON, and Hull, QC: Camden House/Canadian Museum of Civilization, 1994.

Fleming, John, and Michael Rowan. *Folk Furniture of Canada's Doukhobors, Hutterites, Mennonites and Ukranians.* Edmonton, AB: University of Alberta Press, 2004.

Fleming, John A., and Michael J. Rowan. *Canadian Folk Art to 1950.* Edmonton, AB, and Hull, QC: University of Alberta Press and Canadian Museum of Civilization, 2012.

Fleming, Patricia, and Thomas Carpenter. *Traditions in Wood: A History of Wildfowl Decoys in Canada.* Camden East, ON: Camden House, 1987.

Fortin, Real. *Poterie et Vaiselle, Saint-Jean et Iberville.* Saint-Jean-sur-Richelieu, QC: Éditions Mille Roches, 1982.

Fox, Ross. "The Importance of Designer Labels." *ROM Magazine* 44, no. 4 (2012): 6-21.

Frost, Edward Sands. *Edward Sands Frost's Hooked Rug Patterns.* Dearborn, MI: Greenfield Village and Henry Ford Museum, 1970.

Gagnon, François-Marc. *La volière enchantée* ("The Enchanted Aviary"). *Vie des Arts* 20, no. 82 (Spring 1976): 45-49.

Galipeau, Pascale. *Les Paradis du Monde: L'art Populaire du Québec*. Hull, QC: Musée Canadien des Civilisations, 1995.

Gates, B. "Ontario Decoys." *Upper Canadian*, 1982.

Glenbow Museum. *The Spirit Sings: Artistic Traditions of Canada's First Peoples*. Toronto: McClelland and Stewart, 1987.

Grosbois, Louise de, Raymonde Lamothe, and Lise Nantel. *Les Patenteux du Québec*. Montreal: Les Éditions Parti Pris, 1978.

Guyette, Dale and Gary. *Decoys of Maritime Canada*. Exton, PA: Schiffer Publishing, 1983.

Hardy, Jean Pierre. *Arts Populaire du Québec*. Quebec: Musée du Québec, 1975.

Harper, J. Russell. *Early Painters and Engravers in Canada*. Toronto: University of Toronto Press, 1970.

–––. *Painting in Canada: a History*, Toronto: University of Toronto Press, 1974.

–––. *A People's Art: Naïve, Primitive, Provincial, and Folk Art in Canada*. Toronto: University of Toronto Press, 1974.

Harper, J. Russell, Joan Murray, Ralph Price, and Patricia Price. *'Twas Ever Thus, A Selection of Eastern Ontario Folk Art*. Toronto: M.F. Feheley, 1979.

Hemphill, Herbert W., Jr., and Julia Weissman. *Twentieth Century American Folk Art and Artists*. New York: E.P. Dutton, 1974.

Hornung, Clarence P. *Treasury of American Design and Antiques*. New York: Harry N. Abrams, 1970.

Hutchins, Donna and Nigel. *The Maple Leaf Forever: A Celebration of Canadian Symbols*. Erin, ON: Boston Mills, 2006.

Jouvancourt, Hugues de. *Cornelius Krieghoff*. Toronto: Musson Book Company, 1971.

Kettell, Russell Hawes. *The Pine Furniture of Early New England*. New York: Dover Publications, 1929.

Klamkin, Charles. *Weather Vanes: The History, Manufacture and Design of an American Folk Art*. New York and Toronto: Hawthorne Books and Prentice-Hall, 1973.

Kobayashi, Terry, Michael Bird, and Elizabeth Price. *Folk Treasures of Historic Ontario*. Toronto: The Ontario Heritage Foundation, 1985.

Laframboise, Yves. *Intérieurs Québécois: Ambience et décor de nos belles maisons*. Montreal: Les Éditions de l'Homme, 2003.

Langdon, John E. *Canadian Silversmiths 1700-1900*. Toronto: Stinehour Press, 1966.

Lessard, Michel, *Encyclopédie des antiquités du Québec*. Montreal: Les Éditions de l'Homme, 1971.

–––. *Meubles anciens du Québec, quatre siècles de création*. Montreal: Les Éditions de l'Homme, 1999.

–––. *Objets anciens du Québec. La vie domestique*. Montréal: Les Éditions de l'Homme, 1994.

Levasseur, Adrien. *Sculpteurs en art populaire au Québec*. Quebec: Les Éditions GID, 2008.

–––. *Sculptures en art populaire au Québec, tome 2*. Quebec: Les Éditions GID, 2012.

Lipman, Jean. *American Folk Art in Wood, Metal and Stone*. New York: Dover, 1972.

Lipman, Jean, and Alice Winchester. *The Flowering of American Folk Art, 1776-1876*. New York: Viking Press/Whitney Museum of American Art, 1974.

MacDonald, George F. *Haida Art*. Gatineau, QC: Canadian Museum of Civilization, 1982.

MacLaren, George. *Antique Furniture by Nova Scotia Craftsmen*. Toronto: Ryerson Press, 1961.

McKendry, Blake. *Folk Art: Primitive and Naïve Art in Canada*. Toronto: Methuen, 1983.

McKendry, Ruth. *Quilts and Other Bed Coverings in the Canadian Tradition*. Toronto: Van Nostrand Reinhold, 1979.

Newlands, David L. *Early Ontario Potters: Their Craft and Trade*. Toronto/Montreal: McGraw-Hill Ryerson, 1979.

Nutting, Wallace. *Furniture of the Pilgrim Century*. New York: Dover Reprint, 1965.

———. *Furniture Treasury*. Two volumes. New York: Macmillan, 1928.

Pain, Howard. *The Heritage of Upper Canadian Furniture: A Study in the Survival of Formal and Vernacular Styles from Britain, America and Europe, 1780-1900*. Toronto: Van Nostrand Reinhold, 1978.

Palardy, Jean. *The Early Furniture of French Canada*. Toronto: Macmillan, 1963.

Parkman, Francis. *Francis Parkman's Works*. Vols. 11-13: *Montcalm and Wolfe*. Cambridge, MA: Harvard University Press/John Wilson and Son, 1884.

Phillips, Ruth B. *Patterns of Power: The Jasper Grant Collection and Great Lakes Indian Art of the Early Nineteenth Century*. Kleinburg, ON: McMichael Canadian Collection, 1984.

———. *Trading Identities: The Souvenir in Native North American Art from the Northeast, 1700-1900*. Montreal and Kingston/Seattle: McGill-Queen's Univerity Press/University of Washington Press, 1998.

Porter John R., and Jean Bélisle. *La sculpture ancienne au Québec, trios siècles d'art religieux et profane*. Montreal: Les Éditions de l'Homme, 1986.

Profil de la sculpture Québécoise, XVII^c-XIX^c siècle. Québec: Musée du Québec, 1969.

Powers, Steven. *North American Burl Treen: Colonial & Native American*. Self-published, 2005.

Raible, Chris. *From Hands Now, Striving to be Free — Boxes Crafted by 1837 Rebellion Prisoners: An Analysis and Inventory of 94 Boxes*. Toronto: York Pioneer and Historical Society, 2009.

Rasonyi, Lydia Imreh. *La céramique Québécoise ancienne*. Quebec: Ministère des affaires culturelles, 1981.

Sack, Albert. *Fine Points of Furniture: Early American*. Rev. Ed. New York: Crown Publishers, 1986.

Santore, Charles. *The Windsor Style in North America, Volumes I and II*. Philadelphia: Courage Books, 1997.

Schultze, Thomas. *Frances Anne Hopkins: Images from Canada*. Manotick, ON: Penumbra Press, 2008.

Seguin, Robert-Lionel. *Les jouets anciennes du Québec*. Ottawa: Les Éditions Leméac, 1969

Shackleton, Philip. *The Furniture of Old Ontario*. Toronto: Macmillan of Canada, 1978.

Simard, Jean. *Les Arts Sacrés au Québec*. Boucherville, QC: Les Éditions de Mortagne, 1989.

Simard, Jean, Bernard Genest, Francine Labonté, and René Bouchard. *Pour passer le temps: artistes populaires du Québec*. Quebec: Ministère des affaires culturelles, 1985.

Smith, Jean and Elizabeth. *Collecting Canada's Past*. Scarborough, ON: Prentice-Hall, 1974.

Spendlove, F. St. George. *The Face of Early Canada*. Toronto: Ryerson Press, 1958.

St-Onge, François. *Sculpteurs d'appelants du Québec*. Quebec: Les Éditions GID, 2008.

Symons, Scott. *A Romantic Look at Early Canadian Furniture.* Toronto: McClelland and Stewart, 1971.

Telfer, Carol E. *Art of the Grenfell Mission, the Robin Moore Collection.* Collingwood, ON: Michael Donovan, 2000.

Tilney, Phil. *This Other Eden: Canadian Folk Art Outdoors.* Vancouver: Douglas & McIntyre for Canadian Museum of Civilization, 1999.

Treasures of American Folk Art from the Collection of the Museum of American Folk Art. New York: Harry N. Abrams, 1979.

Varkaris, Jane, and James E. Connell. *Early Canadian Timekeepers.* Toronto: Stoddart, 1993.

Vincent, Gilbert T., Sherry Brydon, and Ralph T. Coe, eds. *Art of the North American Indians: The Thaw Collection.* Cooperstown, NY: Fenimore Art Museum, New York State Historical Association, and University of Washington Press, 2000.

Webster, Donald B. *Early Canadian Pottery.* Toronto: McClelland and Stewart, 1971.

———. *Early Slip-Decorated Pottery in Canada.* Toronto: Charles J. Musson, 1969.

———. *Rococo to Rustique, Early French-Canadian Furniture in the Royal Ontario Museum.* Toronto: Royal Ontario Museum, 2000.

Webster, Donald, ed. *The Book of Canadian Antiques.* Toronto: McGraw-Hill Ryerson, 1974.

Weld, Isaac Jr. *Travels through the States of North America and the Provinces of Upper and Lower Canada during the Years 1795, 1796, and 1797.* Picadilly: John Stockdale, 1799.

Wendel, Bruce & Doranna. *Gameboards of North America.* New York: E.P. Dutton with Museum of American Folk Art, 1988.

Whitehead, Ruth Holmes. *Micmac Quillwork: Micmac Indian Techniques of Porcupine Quill Decoration, 1650-1950.* Halifax: Nova Scotia Museum, 1982.

PERIODICALS/MAGAZINES/OTHER

Bowmanville catalogue. *The April Antiques and Folk Art Show, a catalogue by Mel Shakespeare*, 1975.

———. 20th Anniversary, Bowmanville April Antiques Show. Forbes/Gadsden/Lambert, 1993.

Canadian Antiques and Vintage magazine. www.canadianantiquesandvintage.com.

Canadian Museum of History – *Nettie Covey Sharpe.*

www.historymuseum.ca/cmc/exhibitions/arts/art-quebec/art-quebec5_0-e.shtml

www.historymuseum.ca/cmc/exhibitions/arts/sharpe/sharpe_e.shtml

Ornamentum – Decorative Arts in Canada. Toronto. www.ornamentum.ca

Index

Page numbers in *italics* indicate the presence of photos.

Abenaki, *65*, 72, *73–75*
Acomb, Merlin, 152
Adam period, 24, 128
Alves, William, 66, *67*
American Folk Sculpture (Bishop), 102
American, 15–16, 42, 84
Ancienne Lorette, *26–27*
antiques, affordability of, 17–18, 104, 109, 142, 160, 224

Baillargé, Thomas, 84
Barnjum, Frederick Samuel, *30–37*
Barnjum, Helen, 34
Bartlett, Martha, 12
beaver, *25*, 104, *105*, *218–19*
Berlinguet, François-Xavier, 84
Bernier, Joseph Romuald, 102, *103*
birch bark
    canoe model, *144–45*
    canoes, 106, 108
    quillwork, *20*, *28–29*, 114
bird decoys, *176*, *180–85*
birds
    by Bernier, J.R., 102, *103*
    carved on shelves, *162*
    by Côté, J.B., *88–93*
    Manitoba pheasant carving, *214–15*
    parrot on a speckled roost, *90–93*
    peep decoy (sandpiper), *183*
    plovers, *181–82*
    red knot decoy, *182*
    by Richard, Damase, 58, *59*
    Seminary parrot, 15, 120, *121*

thunderbird motif, 60, *61*
weathervane, 40, *41*
yellowlegs, *176*, *180–81*, *185*
Bishop, Robert: *American Folk Sculpture*, 102
Bonaventure Antique Show, 15
Bourgault, Jacques, *176*, *186–87*
Bourguet, Gerard, 12
Bowmanville Antiques and Folk Art Show, 60, 120
boxes
    Abenaki deed, *65*, 72, *73–75*
    convent, *14*, *110*, *114–18*
    deed box, *10*
    Huron, 112, *113*
    Mi'kmaq, *119*
    Newfoundland keepsake, *96–97*
    rebellion, 66, *67*
British Columbia, First Nations motifs, 60, *61*
Burney family rug, 210, *211*

Campobello Island, 220, 222
Canada General Service Medal, *223*
Canadian Folk Art to 1950 (Fleming & Rowan), 12, 60
Canadian Museum of History, 90–91, *93*, 126, 160, 227
Canadian Scenery — Le paysage canadien, 106
Canning, Nova Scotia, 138
canoe paddle, 140, *141*
card table, *76–79*
carved bowl, *176*, *179*
carved brush, *68–71*
carving techniques
    chip carving, 112, 116
    Friesian, 112, 116, 118

chairs
    deck chairs, *221*
    French Régime, 15, *38*, *42–45*
    John Tulles, *80–81*
    Scottish, *20*, *28–29*
chandelier, 15, *110*, 122, *123*
chantecler weathervane, 40, *41*, *53*
Chapelle Notre Dame de Lorette, 26
Charleson, J.B., 140, *141*
Charters, Edward, 126
Chase, William, 138
Chestnut, Robert, *207–09*
Chestnut Hardware and Chestnut Canoe Company, 208–09
Chippendale style, 16, 24
collecting, 17–19
collections
    Adrien Flibotte, 188
    Canadian Museum of History, 72, 91, *93*, 126
    Charles Goodfellow, 218
    Emily Lebaron, 102
    George & Louise Richardson, 64
    Glenbow Museum, 70
    Marjorie McConnell, 182, *183*
    Musée de l'Hôtel Dieu, 112
    Musée national des beaux-arts du Québec, 137
    Nettie Sharpe, 58, 70, 72, 90–91, *93*, 102
    Ralph and Patricia Price, 50
    Wiser Distillery Canadiana, 168
commemorative images, 21
    commemorative rug, *149*
    John A. Macdonald plate, *21*
construction techniques, 44, 52, 66, 72, 80, 112, 128, *129*, 181

convent boxes, *14, 110, 114–18*
Côté, Jean-Baptiste, *84–85, 87–94*
crooked knife, 104, *105*
cupboards
    Louis XV armoire, *127,*
      128, *129*
    maple, 64, *65*
    Neoclassic, 24

Death of Wolfe (painting), *62–63,*
    98–99
deck chairs, *221*
decorating, 72, 126
decoys
    hollow-bodied, *184*
    peep decoy, *183*
    PEI golden plover, *181*
    red knot, *182*
    Toronto plover decoy, *182*
    yellowlegs, *185*
    yellowlegs root head, *181*
Decoys of Maritime Canada
    (Guyette & Guyette), *181*, 185
deer carving, *135, 168–69*
desks
    slant front desk, *135, 221*
    Thomas Nisbet legislative,
      154, *155*
diamond point, 22, *23, 52–53,* 128
diamond point doors, 22, *23*
display arrangements, 72, 126,
    176, 207
Dobson, Henry, 12, 86
Doyle, S.J., *111, 124–25*
draught horses, *38, 48–51*
dressing tables, *158–59*
drum table, *38,* 46, *47*
Dundas, Ontario, *54–55*

Early Furniture of French Canada,
    The (Palardy), 17
Early Painters and Engravers of
    Canada (Harper), 30
Enfield rifle, 220, *221–22*

Fenian raids, *220–23*
First Nations motifs
    Abenaki, 72, *73–75*

carved brush, *68–71*
crooked knife, 104, *105*
Huron, 112, *113*
Mi'kmaq, *18, 28–29, 68–71,*
    114–16, 119
West Coast, 60, *61*
First World War posters, *224–25*
Fitzpatrick, Deanne, *206,* 207,
    210–13
Fleming, John A.: *Canadian Folk*
    Art to 1950, 12, 60; *The Painted*
    Furniture of French Canada, 120
Folk Art — Primitive and Naive Art
    in Canada (McKendry), 114, 118,
    143, 166
Fort Duquesne, *132, 133*
Fox, Ross, 78
French Régime Armchair, 15, *38,*
    42–45, 132–33
fruit vendor sign, *110,* 111, *130–31*

Gagnon, Clarence, 136, *137,* 144
Gale, Denis, *174–75*
game boards, 96, *97, 132–33, 177,*
    188–205
Garon, Magloire, 152
Grenfell Mission, 142, 144
guns, 220, *221–22*
Guyette, Dale: *Decoys of Maritime*
    Canada, 181, 185
Guyette, Gary: *Decoys of Maritime*
    Canada, 181, 185

Halifax dressing table, *158–59*
Harper, J. Russell: *Early Painters*
    and Engravers of Canada, 30
Heise, Phoebe, *149*
Hepplewhite style, 16, 152, 178
Heritage Furnishings of Atlantic
    Canada (Dobson & Dobson),
    86, 100
Hill, John, 82
hinges, 22, *23,* 24, *52,* 128
Holland Landing, *82–83*
hollow-bodied decoy, *184*
hooked rugs. *See* rugs
Hopkins, Frances Anne, 106, *107*
horse and buggy carving, 160, *161*

horse pull toys, *216–17*
horses
    carvings of, 38, *48–51,* 160, *161,*
      216–17
    paintings of, *30–37*
Hümme, Julius, *166–67*
Huron box, 112, *113*
Hutchins, E.J., *170–71*

ice fishing lure, *16*
International Hotel, *111, 124–25*
iron beds, *135,* 168

J.J. and D. Howe company deck
    chairs, *221*
Jobin, Louis, 90
Josefina, *155,* 156, *157*
Joyal, Maria Laplante, 146, *147–48*

Krieghoff, Cornelius, 30, *174–75*

La volière enchantée ("The
    Enchanted Aviary"), 90
Lachine, Quebec, 106
Laurentian Village rug, 136, *137*
Laurier, Sir Wilfrid, *20–21*
LeClercq, Chrestien, 68
legislative desk, 154, *155*
L'habitant sculpture, *84–85,* 87
Longpré, A., *162–63*
Louis XV armoire, *127,* 128, *129*
Lount, Samuel, 82

Macdonald, John A., 66
    commemorative plate, *20–21*
McGee table, 95, *100–101*
Mackenzie, Alexander, 108, *109*
Mackenzie, William Lyon, 66, 82
Madilla Smith, 15, *150–51, 153*
Mahar, J.A., *111, 124–25*
Manitoba
    pheasant carving, *214–15*
    Winnipeg painting, *170–71*
McKendry, Blake: *Folk Art —*
    Primitive and Naive Art in Canada,
    114, 118, 143, 166
Mi'kmaq objects, *18,* 20, *28–29,*
    68–71, 114, *119*

models
  canoe, *144–45*
  Holland Landing Red Mill,
    82–83
  timber shanty, *135, 164–65*, 168
mortar and pestle, *12*
Musée national des beaux-arts du
  Québec, 136, *137*

naive
  as a style, *96, 100, 143, 146, 156,
    172, 181*
  carved deed box, *10*
  construction and carving
    techniques, 21, 26, 72, 138
Napoleon sculpture, *126, 127*
native figures, paintings of, *174–75*
Neoclassic style, 24, *25*
New Brunswick
  Chestnut, Robert, *207–09*
  deck chairs, *221*
  Enfield rifle, 220, *221–22*
  Legislative desk, 154, *155*
  Napoleon sculpture, *126–27*
  "Nisbet" sewing table, *86–87*
  slant front desk, *135, 221*
  Stevens Family portraits,
    94–95
Niagara Falls, *38, 39, 48–49*, 110
Nipawin, Robin, *214–15*
Nisbet, Thomas, 76, *86–87,* 154,
  155, 158
Nova Scotia
  card table, *76–78*
  furniture styles in, 16
  Halifax dressing table, *158–59*
  McGee table, *100–01*
  rugs by Fitzpatrick, D., *206,
    207, 210–13*
  side chair, *80–81*
  Silas Patterson heart table,
    138–39
  Trapunto Rug, *143*
  yellowlegs root head decoy, *181*

oil paintings
  by Barnjum, F., *30–34*
  Chestnut, Robert, *207–09*

Death of Wolfe (painting),
  62–63, 98–99
  by Hümme, J., *166–67*
  Madilla Smith, 15, *150–51, 153*
  by Seavey, J.R., *54–55*
  Stevens Family portraits,
    94–95
  by Whale, R., *38, 39, 48–49*
  See also watercolour paintings
Ontario
  1837 rebellion box, 66, *67*
  decorated canoe paddle, 140, *141*
  Holland Landing Red Mill
    model, *82–83*
  horse and buggy carving,
    160, *161*
  Madilla Smith, 15, *150–51, 153*
  Norfolk county buffet, 178, *179*
  painting by Hümme, J., *166–67*
  peep decoy, *183*
  red knot decoy, *182*
  timber shanty model, *135,
    164–65*, 168
  Toronto plover decoy, *182*

*Painted Furniture of French Canada,
  The* (Fleming), 120
paintings. *See* oil paintings;
  watercolour paintings
Palardy, Jean: *The Early Furniture
  of French Canada*, 17
parallel rule, *207, 208–09*
*Parrot on a Speckled Roost,
  90–91, 93*
Patterson, Silas, 138
peep decoy, *183*
PEI golden plover decoy, *181*
Pelletier, Joseph, 21
pickers, 22, 56, 146, 162
"Portneuf" pottery, *24–25*
portraits
  Chestnut, Robert, *207–09*
  Josefina, *155, 156, 157*
  Madilla Smith, 15, *150–51, 153*
  Stevens family, *94–95, 101*
posters, *224–25*
Prince Edward Island
  golden plover decoy, *181*

hollow-bodied, *184*
  yellowlegs, *185*
Princess of Wales' Own Regiment
  (PWOR), 223
prisoner boxes, 66, *67*
Provincial Elegance, A (Dobson &
  Dobson), 86

Quebec
  Abenaki deed boxes, *65, 72,
    73–75*
  Ancienne Lorette walking
    stick, *26–27*
  beaver weathervane, *218–19*
  Bernier, Joseph R., 102, *103*
  carved brush, *68–71*
  carved deer, *139, 168–69*
  chandeliers, 15, *110, 122, 123*
  diamond point armoire,
    52–53, 128
  draught horse carvings, 38,
    49–51
  drum table, 38, 46, *47*
  French Régime armchair, 15,
    38, *42–45*
  fruit vendor sign, *110, 111,
    130–31*
  furniture styles in, 16
  game boards, *177, 190–205*
  Huron box, 112, *113*
  Laurentian Village rug,
    136, *137*
  L'habitant carving, *84–85*, 87
  Little Jack Horner bakery
    trade sign, *176, 186–87*
  Longpré bird shelf, *162*
  Louis XV armoire, *127*, 128,
    129
  maple corner cupboard, 64, *65*
  Neoclassic corner cupboard,
    20, 24–25
  Parcheesi game board, *188–89*
  rugs by Joyal, M.L., 146, *147–48*
  steamship painting, *172–73*
  weathervane, 40, *41*
  See also Côté, Jean-Baptiste;
    Richard, Damase
Quebec chest of drawers, *152–53*

quillwork
    birch bark canoe model, *144–45*
    Mi'kmaq, *18, 20, 28–29*, 114

Ramsay, John, *184*
rebellion boxes, 66, *67*
recruitment posters, *224–25*
red knot decoy, *182*
refinished objects, 24. *See also* restoration
Regency style, 154, *155*
research sources, 17
restoration, 52
Rhéaume, Damase, 84
Richard, Damase, 84
    carved bird, 58, *59*
    carved cat, 38, *56–57*, 58
    carved squirrel, *58*
rifles, 220, *221–22*
Robert Whale, *38, 39*
Robinson, Peter, 82
Rogerson, John, 126
rooster carving, *88–89*
Roth, Jacob, 160, *161*
Rowan, Michael: *Canadian Folk Art to 1950*, 12, 60
Rowlings, William, *181*
Roy, Phillipe, 84
rugs
    Burney family, 210, *211*
    by Fitzpatrick, D., *206*, 207, *210–13*
    flying mallards, *144–45*
    hooking process, 142
    by Joyal, M.L., 146, *147–48*
    Laurentian Village, 136, *137*
    Nova Scotia Trapunto, *143*

Queen Elizabeth's coronation, *149*

Saco-Biddeford Carver, 102, *103*
sandpiper decoy, *183*
Seavey, Julian Ruggles, *54–55*
Seminary Parrot, 15, 120, *121*
Sexton, Ezekiel, 15, *150–51*
Sharpe, Nettie, 56, 72, 90–91, 93, 146, *227–28*
    collection, 58, 72, 90–91, 93, 102
Sheraton style, 16, 76, 86, 138, *139*
ship model, *207–08*
shorebird carvings, 176, *180–85*
signs
    fruit vendor, *110*, 111, *130–31*
    International Hotel, *111*, *124–25*
    Little Jack Horner bakery, 176, *186–87*
Sir Wilfrid Laurier (statue), *20–21*
slant front desk, *135*, 221
Southam, Thomas, *182–83*

tables
    drum style, 46, *47*
    John Tulles table, *76–79*
    McGee, 95, *100–101*
    Silas Patterson heart, *138–39*
telescope, *207*, 209
Toronto plover decoy, *182*
toys. *See* horse pull toys; game boards
Trade signs
    fruit vendor, *110*, 111, *130–31*
    International Hotel, *111*, *124–25*
    Little Jack Horner bakery, 176, *186–87*

Tremblay, Georges-Édouard, 142
Tulles, John
    chair by, *80–81*
    Halifax dressing table, *158–59*
    table by, *76–79*

Upper Canadian, 152
U.S.
    cross-border behaviours, 124
    items found in, 15, *42*, 120, 136, *137*, 220, *221–22*

voyageur style canoe model, *144–45*

walking sticks, Ancienne Lorette, *26–27*
wall art, 144. *See also* paintings; rugs
watercolour paintings
    by Barnjum, F., *35*
    by Gale, D., *174–75*
    by Hopkins, F.A., 106, *107*
    by Hümme, J., 166
    by Hutchins, E.J., *170–71*
    S.S. *Quebec* (steamship), *172–73*
    See also oil paintings
weathervanes
    beaver, *218–19*
    rooster, 40, *41, 53*
Weld, Isaac, 108, *109*
Whale, Robert, *38, 39, 48–49*
Wiser Distillery Canadiana collection, 168

yellowlegs decoys, *181, 185*